BABAJI'S KRIYA YOGA
Deepening Your Practice

By

Jan Ahlund

&

Marshall Govindan

Babaji's Kriya Yoga and Publications, Inc
St. Etienne de Bolton, Quebec, Canada

Babaji's Kriya Yoga : Deepening Your Practice
By Jan Ahlund and Marshall Govindan

First published in August 2009 by
Babaji's Kriya Yoga and Publications, Inc.
196 Mountain Road, P.O. Box 90
Eastman, Quebec, Canada J0E 1P0
Telephone: 450-197-0258 or 1-888-252-9642; fax: 1-450-297-3957
www.babajiskriyayoga.net email: info@babajiskriyayoga.net

Cover design and graphic layout by David Lavoie
Drawings by Barbara Miller. Photographs by Marshall Govindan

Printed and bound in Canada

Library and Archives Canada Cataloguing in Publication

Ahlund, Jan Suzanne
        Babaji's Kriya Yoga: Deepening Your Practice / by
                Ahlund, Jan and Govindan, Marshall

ISBN: 978-1-895383-64-5

        1. Yoga, Kriya. I. Govindan, Marshall II. Title.

BL1238.56.K74A44 2009   294.5'436   C2009-905168-0

Table of Contents

Introduction

The tradition of Babaji's Kriya Yoga is a classical form of Yoga. It flows directly from the ancient Kriya tradition of South India, from perfected masters of Siva Yoga, known as the Eighteen Siddhas. However, Babaji's Kriya Yoga also has Himalayan Siddha roots, as the techniques can be traced back to the Maha Siddha Kriya Babaji, the legendary Satguru of Paramahamsa Yogananda and written about in his masterpiece, *Autobiography of a Yogi*. The number of South Indian Siddhas (eighteen) might be considered merely symbolic of the teachings or of the eighteen mystical states of consciousness. The book, *The Yoga of the Eighteen Siddhas: An Anthology (2004)*, does however provide us with a glimpse of the teachings of the eighteen Siddhas in verse, and reveals some details about the early life of two great Siddhas, Agastyar and Boganathar, who were said to have been the principle gurus of Kriya Babaji. (See *Babaji and the Eighteen Siddha Kriya Yoga Tradition*).

Three books of teachings on Kriya Yoga were dictated by Siddha Babaji in 1952 and 1953, to a disciple, V.T Neelakantan, and have been reprinted and published with the title *The Voice of Babaji: Triology on Kriya Yoga (2003)*. These writings along with one additional book, *Man, Life, Death and After (1954)*, reveal the early years of a new mission, which Babaji started through his disciples V.T Neelakatan and S.A.A. Ramaiah. Babaji taught to Yogi Ramaiah a synthesis of what he learned from his gurus, in a progressive system of techniques, 144 kriyas, which they referred to as Babaji's Kriya Yoga. There is a certain authority and genuineness in these techniques of Kriya Yoga, a sense of sacredness, superbness and purity, which makes them feel "untouched by human hand."

Babaji's Kriya Yoga is an authentic and complete system of 144 techniques, which bring about awareness and Self-realization. It is a system of Raja Yoga (royal path) based on directing the *prana* (life force) to purify and balance the mind and emotions. The system is a five-fold path:

1) **Kriya Hatha Yoga** - physical postures that produce relaxation and stability;

2) **Kriya Kundalini Pranayama** - breathing techniques to awaken and circulate one's potential power and consciousness throughout the chakras, or psycho-energetic centers;

3) **Kriya Dhyana Yoga** - the scientific art of mastering the mind through various concentration and meditation techniques to cleanse the subconscious and to develop inner senses and the power to visualize and manifest what one is seeking in life;

4) **Kriya Mantra Yoga** - the silent, mental repetition of particular sounds to awaken the intellect to higher levels of consciousness and creative intelligence and to purify the subconscious of its habits, or *samskaras*;

5) **Kriya Bhakti Yoga** - the cultivation of divine love and spiritual aspiration for the True, the Good, the Beautiful the surrender of the ego bound consciousness to that of one's highest Self. When the soul sincerely calls for liberation from the ego's desires and aversions, Grace responds in the form of spiritual experiences.

In addition to these five Yogas, both Raja Yoga and Babaji's Kriya Yoga describe other necessary steps: *yamas, niyamas, pratyahara* and *Samadhi*. The *yamas* can be defined as restraints or the ethical practices of non-violence, truthfulness, non-stealing, sensual restraint and greedlessness. *Niyamas* are the principles of personal behavior or self-discipline. These consist of the observances of contentment (*santosha*), purity (*shaucha*), self-study (*svadhyaya*), intense practice (*tapas*), and surrender to the Lord (*Ishvara pranidhana*). These are lifestyle principles necessary to establish a personal yogic practice in life. *Pratyahara* is a withdrawal of consciousness from the senses, from the sensations of sound, sight, touch, taste, and smell. It is a withdrawal of the sensory impressions, which limit the mind. It is the ability to be undisturbed by noise and turmoil in your environment, so that you can meditate. It also includes withdrawal from the wrong foods and the wrong associations or relationships in life. *Pratyahara* comes naturally in all five of the Kriya Yogas. *Samadhi*, the breathless state of awareness or cognitive is the deepest meditation in which you are absorbed in the object of your awareness. While there are various levels of *Samadhi*, you ultimately become "aware of That which is aware." There is direct perception of the ultimate reality. It may result from an intense practice of meditation. Kriya Yoga trains one in specific *Samadhi* techniques.

Babaji's Kriya Yoga is a proven system that develops one's capacity in all five planes of existence: physical, vital (emotional), mental, intellectual and spiritual. These Kriya Yoga techniques function in an integral manner to secure for the practitioner vibrant health and vitality, cheerfulness, mental clarity and compassion. Sense perceptions become keen and clear, and the mind and the intellect are wonderfully sharpened. Latent faculties are developed and personal power is increased. However, these are not developed for purposes of limited self interest, but as a means of serving the expanded sense of Self, found in others. Compassion and intuition grow, along with the capacity to serve. And as one's consciousness expands, the needs of others are recognized as one's own.

Kriya Yoga is a practical art and science of realizing your full potential here in this world. It requires no adherence to any religious belief system. It does not matter if you are a Christian, a Buddhist, or a Hindu, an agnostic or an atheist. Anyone can benefit from its practice. Kriya Yoga is "action with awareness," and through it, you will experience awareness and learn to take that awareness actively into everyday living. In addition, you can attain significantly improved and robust physical health, increased vital energy, mental clarity, heightened intuitive faculties, Self awareness, and spiritual joy, peace and well being.

Chapter 1

Action with Awareness

Action with awareness is both the vehicle and the destination in Babaji's Kriya Yoga. Through it we become aware of *That which is aware;*" which is the one constant underlying all of our thoughts and experiences.

Yoga was originally developed in India as a spiritual path of Self-realization; however, today it enjoys worldwide popularity due to its many practical benefits. The passage of this physical/spiritual discipline, from an ancient Indian culture to a modern western culture, has yet to reconcile the values inherent in each culture. Yoga is most often taught as a system of physical exercises to improve health or, minimally in some cases, to reduce and tighten the body. As a result, westernized Yoga is often only a pale shadow of what it truly can be. Fortunately, there are a growing number of teachers in the West who are attempting to co-join the practice of asana with pranayama and meditation to take students deeper into the goals of Yoga. This trend is welcome indeed, but even where one is instructed to be aware of the breath or alignment, little is communicated about the nature of consciousness or how to act with awareness, or how to find lasting happiness, which are the true goals of Yoga.

The enlightened and perfected rishis and Siddhas developed the scientific art of Yoga in order to perfect the human condition. The normal human condition is to act with little or no awareness. The Siddhas suggests our dilemma is that "we are dreaming with our eyes open." Human life is dreamlike. Everything comes and goes like dreams: pleasure and pain, success and failure, possessions, relationships, along with the youth of the body. Because we are absorbed in the dream, we act unconsciously, pushed on by instinct, impulse, conditioned habit, desire or aversion.

Ultimately, we are all either seeking happiness or avoiding suffering of one kind or another. Unfortunately, finding happiness is like trying to pick up water with the fingers—it easily slips away. Getting what we want, whether it is pleasure, wealth, power, physical beauty or adoration, inevitably brings about suffering. We suffer in fear of losing what we have, or suffer boredom, restlessness or dissatisfaction with it. Thus, we keep moving from this and that experience to the next in the vain hope of finding lasting happiness, or at least, another diversion. Lasting happiness seems to escape everyone.

Is there no way out of this universal dilemma? Is there a way to find lasting happiness?

The Rishis and Siddhas say "yes," that "the amount of happiness in life is proportional to one's discipline." Discipline, in the context of Yoga, is to **remember who you truly are and to let**

go of identifying with what you are not.   It begins with the cultivation of "awareness."

What is Awareness and how do we acquire it?

Awareness is concentrated consciousness. It is not the same thing as the mind. It is a higher intelligence, which maintains the perspective of detached observation. Awareness occurs when part of our consciousness (our higher discriminating mind) stands back and witnesses what the rest of our waking consciousness is involved in doing, feeling or thinking. This rarely occurs in the ordinary course of life because we usually allow our consciousness to be absorbed by the objects of our attention. We lose "ourselves" in all of the movements of the mind. We either identify with what we are seeing, hearing, thinking, feeling, or doing, or we allow our consciousness to be dispersed in many different directions. We often do things without taking notice of what we are doing. We lose our keys, glasses, cell phone or important paperwork, or overreact and ruin relationships due to inattention to the present moment. Inattention is lack of awareness. Awareness is concentrated, dispassionate attention.

An experience of awareness is being a passive "witness" to the passing show of sensory and emotional movements. This disentangles us from our conditioning, so that we can respond to circumstances from a wider perspective. Awareness is a calm state, which actively engages the mind in the present moment. It is assertive, reasoning intelligence that is capable of making correct judgments and decisions. By regularly overstepping conditioned habitual programming (instinct, impulse, emotion), this higher intelligence is strengthened and detachment and discrimination is honed.

Just being able to clear subjective movements from the surface of the mind does not indicate that we have established a state of Awareness. Awareness opens the mind to the subtle movements active on the more profound levels of our being. This heightened sense of awareness glides us into deep levels of meditation, bringing about a sense of stillness everywhere. Awareness is a state of absolute calmness and stillness, which unveils an indescribable quality of spiritual energy. If we repeatedly allow ourselves to rest inwardly in this state, the mind becomes more concentrated, discriminating, and dispassionate in all situations. The movements of the breath slow and become regulated. The mind is gradually purified of its conditioning and happiness arises naturally in the heart.

What part of me is Aware?

The Siddhas say, "be in the world, but not of it." This is their self-study course for life. Normally, we are conditioned to be absorbed by the objects of our attention: our thoughts, memories, emotions, needs, desires, and aversions. Our tendency is to act in reaction to the pull of the world, without considering the essential existential questions, **"Who is acting?"** and

"Who am I?" We think, talk, act, react, emote, but rarely do we connect with the "I" who is doing these things. We read books and acquire information without considering who is reading or obtaining information. We fall in love without observing to whom this is happening, or we get angry or depressed without really knowing why. We say, "I am in love," "I am angry," "I am depressed," "I believe this or that." We eat, work, exercise and fall asleep, get up and do it all over again as a routine, without ever observing the process. We don't stop the thoughts long enough to ask the question, "who is thinking, acting, emoting, exercising or sleeping or believing?" Yoga enables us to realize the answer to these questions through the cultivation of awareness.

About 200 A.D., Sage Patanjali wrote his classic, *The Yoga Sutras*. In it he makes a clear distinction between that which is conscious, the Seer, versus everything else one experiencs, the Seen, including all of the movements within the mind. The Seer is the Witness, our purely subjective perspective, that which is conscious, that which is experienced as "I am." The Seen is everything else in Nature: all objects of awareness from the most physical of objects to the subtlest of thoughts and mental formations. Mind is the sum of all mental formations, including memory, imagination, sensory input, and intellectual abstractions.

Patanjali defines Yoga in verse 2 of his *Yoga Sutras*, in the following words: **Yogas citta vrtti nirodhah** or "Yoga is the cessation of (the identification with) the fluctuations arising within consciousness." In subsequent verses, Patanjali defines these five fluctuations as: **1)** the means of acquiring true knowledge, which is knowledge validated through our five senses and inference, which is observed cause and effect; **2)** misconception, which is false knowledge based on personal bias; **3)** conceptualization, which is thinking about our experience; **4)** memory, the retention of past experiences; **5)** deep sleep, which is the thought of nothingness. The ego identifies habitually with these five kinds of fluctuations.

Yoga may thus be understood as a systematic process of cleansing consciousness of egoism, the habit of identifying with what you are not. If you are asked, for example, who you are, you typically respond by referring to your name, profession, place of residence and your relationship with someone else. However, these are not constants and indeed often do change. These things with which you identify are readily forgotten each night during sleep. During sleep, you have no recollection of your name, profession, or relationships, yet the sense of "I" continues.

It is the sense of "I" which is truly profound. However, consider what the "I" typically identifies with: fatigue, hunger, boredom, fear, anger, lust, frustration, jealously, envy, need, excitement, happiness, sadness and pain—all that one is feeling, thinking and doing, all of which is constantly changing. But how can you truly be something which is here one moment and gone the next? Can any one of these things really be who you are? Yoga says, what is real, what is true, is "That, which always is." Find that part of you which always is and always will be. That is Yoga.

"The real tragedy of mankind is that man has lost himself."
Kriya Babaji *"Man, Life, Death and After"*

Finding the Real, Unchanging Self

Yoga is a process of discovering the real, unchanging self. It requires one to let go of identifying with what one is not, through the cultivation of awareness. And what is one not? Anything that changes, anything which is temporary. Kriya Yoga techniques systematically strip away false identifications with the unreal to develop awareness of the ever-present self, the one constant, effulgent self awareness. This goal is referred to as "Self-realization." Unlike any form of personal growth, however, it does not concern itself with the personality, or even the development of new skills or abilities. Its aim is to install awareness in the very heart of one's being and establish a wide-perspective in one's mind. Only then is one suitably prepared to act consciously at all times.

"The world is torn asunder with disharmony because man has lost his moorings.
Bewildered because not knowing what he is and what ought to be his goal, man expends his
energy in diverse ways. Once he finds himself he is virtually recreated. Previously a
speck, without purpose, without meaning, once he has found himself, he finds his true
existence in the world. And so stands firm with new poise and new dignity."
Kriya Babaji - *Man, Life, Death and After*

The Process of Self Realization

Self-realization requires us to realize that we are not limited to the physical body or even the intellect. We can transcend even subtle intelligence to find the subtlest consciousness of the Bliss-filled Existence Self. Each of us must come to realize that the "I" within, is in essence the same "I" as in others. Consciousness is One. That is why, what afflicts or delights us, afflicts and delights others. Consequently, our well-being is interspersed with the well-being of those who surround us. Therefore, we must aspire not only for our own good, but also for the good of others.

Surely, such a state of Self-realization is an uncommon state of mind. However, it does occur whenever awareness occurs, whenever there is a simple, non-judgmental witnessing; in other words, when one identifies with the Seer, the one who is seeing, not with that which is being seen. Whenever such awareness occurs, unconditional joy occurs. This can easily be tested by any one of us.

Allow part of your consciousness to go inward, to step back as a silent witness, judging nothing, wanting nothing. Simply be. Become aware of what is happening outside of you. You will notice that a simple contentment arises.

Contentment is unconditional joy. Happiness occurs when we get what we want. Unhappiness occurs when we get what we don't want. Contentment doesn't care. Contentment is self-existent and requires us only to be centered on the Self and apart from the pull of the world around us.

In India the term for Self-realization is *Satchitananda*. *Satchitananda* is also a three part formula for finding joy in life. *"Sat"* means absolute being; *"Chit"* means absolute awareness or consciousness; and *"Ananda"* means absolute joy or bliss. It means that when who you truly are is present, Awareness is present, and with Awareness comes unconditional joy.

Patanjali defines his Yoga as "Kriya Yoga" in *Sutra* II.1, and says that it consists of "constant practice" (*abyasah*), detachment (*vairgya*) and devotion to the Lord, (*Ishvara-pranidhana*). Always coming back to the center, to the Seer, to the moment is constant practice, *"abhyasa."*

Recognizing that few of us are prepared to constantly practice such detachment and devotion, he prescribes some alternative practices, known to many of us as the eightfold path of Raja Yoga. Kriya Yoga is a form of Raja Yoga.

The great Siddha Babaji Nagaraj, a contemporary brother disciple of Patanjali, has brought down to the present time a "Kriya Yoga," which shares much of Patanjali's philosophical and practical teachings. Babaji's Kriya Hatha Yoga, while it may be practiced simply for improving one's health, cannot be fully understood or even appreciated without knowing how it relates to other branches of Kriya Yoga, including meditation and breathing, and the ultimate objective of Self-realization.

Realization is the ultimate goal, but the world has gone through a cycle of tremendous changes in its ideas and modes of life. Babaji repeatedly says in *The Voice of Babaji*, that today our goal should be a life of activity in the spirit of selflessness without expectation of any return or reward. Selfless service, he tells us, is the Yoga most suitable for the emancipation of the world, as well as for the individual as it brings about ethical perfection.

In Babaji's own words, "it is possible for every one of you to become a kriya yogi, if only you would not yield to the dictates of your lower self and would abandon conceit. The aspirant has to bear in mind that impurities of egoism, of the human personality, such as anger and ambition, will stop progress in its tracks. No one who is subject to assaults of anger, whatever the reason, or who is ambitious of name, fame and power, can be a true kriya yogi. Whenever anger arises from within, turn to Silence. Whenever anger confronts you, turn to mental silence, discriminative knowledge and the Eternal Self." (*Man, Life, Death and After*)

Can the Self be realized through Kriya Yoga?

The answer is an emphatic "yes." Kriya Yoga is an integral science. It aims at a thorough transformation and integration of every side of life, through the magical touch of higher consciousness. Kriya Yoga is a means of attuning oneself with the Infinite at every step, at every stage of life. Even at the most fundamental stage of the yoga practice, there are transformative powers available, for the glory of one's true self is the metaphysical entity abiding within the very heart of the physical, vital, and intellectual being.

As the self and the Supreme Self come nearer, the hand of the Lord is felt in the arrangements of life. One begins to feel in tune with one's soul, or with the universe, or has the sweet satisfaction of being a co-creator in one's personal destiny. One begins to establish a perpetual relationship with one's true being and begins humbly to serve others, even in the most mundane work, with efficiency, effectiveness and love. One experiences a sense of grace in one's life. This is the meaning and goal of Babaji's Kriya Yoga.

Chapter 2
Babaji's Kriya Hatha Yoga

What is Hatha Yoga?

"Asana should be practiced for gaining steady posture, health and suppleness of the body. With the mastery of each asana, the body and the mind both experience a rebirth." (**Swami Swatmarama**, *Hatha Yoga Pradipika,* **15th Century**)

Babaji's Kriya Hatha Yoga aims at preparing the body, especially the nervous system and the mind for higher spiritual practices. Those who believe that the practice of Hatha Yoga, including asana (physical postures), is only for physical development are misinformed and overlook the scope of its benefits. The human body is not just made of flesh and bones. It is also a powerful vehicle of consciousness and energy. The practice of asana is very important for a spiritual aspirant in order to awaken his dormant spiritual and psychic faculties. Although asanas lead to the spiritual path, they themselves may or may not yield spiritual realization.

Kriya Hatha Yoga utilizes physical movement and concentration. Postures practiced in coordination with the breath can eliminate excesses of both inertia and restlessness in the body and mind. A few asanas practiced in a slow and non-competitive way, with proper breathing and concentration can develop awareness. A state of awareness occurs naturally as the breath is regulated and deepens, inertia and restless is eliminated, brain activity slows and the senses turn inward. Perfecting the practice of asana, can be a vehicle to human perfection if one's goal is not performance oriented, but is instead focused on self discovery.

Kriya Yoga is a Total Hygiene

Kriya Hatha Yoga is a total hygiene that takes into account complete purification of the entire organism. We have not only a physical body, but four more subtle sheaths or bodies: the vital body, which is the seat of our emotions, desires and impulses to act; the mental body, that dimension in which we dream, fantasize, remember and organize the experiences coming from our five senses; the intellectual body, which is even more subtle, where we experience abstract reasoning and insight; the spiritual body, that most subtle dimension, where the Witness within pure, unchanging consciousness, lies. The practice of physical postures can involve all five of these bodies in an integral, synergistic manner. The subtle bodies are a bridge between the physical and our spiritual dimension. They are the means by which the physical body can access spiritual power, light and true knowledge.

A Path to the Spiritual Self

Kriya Hatha Yoga is the path of realizing this true inner spiritual self through physical and mental development. A person may come to a Kriya Hatha Yoga class with only one goal in mind, for example, relief of back pain. Relaxing and strengthening back muscles, overcoming functional disorders like asthma, diabetes or hypertension, working on thyroid problems, or even losing weight are good reasons to begin Hatha Yoga, and these are relatively easy to correct. However, Kriya Hatha Yoga can develop the mental and spiritual faculties of the practitioner who does not want only the therapeutic benefits. The postures can purify and energize the body and calm and master the mind if one practices them with concentration on the breath and the psychic centers (*chakras*) in the vital body.

The *chakras* are subtle, spiritual centers of energy found along the axis of the body. They are coincident with various nerve plexus along the spinal cord in the physical body, however, they are a plexus of subtle, activated, positive and negative energies called *nadis*. The centers on this subtle central axis are ever-changing due to the vital life energy (prana, the bioplasm of life) flowing through them. The Siddhas described the spinning centers as wheels, lotuses, balls, or eggs and called them *adharas* (supports, thresholds or spiritual gates), the only true *chakra* being the seventh center at the crown of the head, the *Sahasrara* (thousand-petalled lotus, place of transcendence). Sahasrara is the destination, not a step along the way.

Each of these centers is a storehouse of vital energy and consciousness. If we meditate deeply on these centers along the spine, they can become stimulated and in turn awaken latent potential and provide us with opportunities to master the mind and senses and experience higher planes of consciousness. The six *adharas* linked in one central line, reflecting certain forms of consciousness are: *muladhara* found at the perineum, at base of the *sushumna nadi*; *svadhisthana* at the sacrum; *manipura*, found behind the navel; *anahata*, behind the physical heart; *vishuddhi*, in the throat; *ajna*, forehead center, midbrain. It seems the most authentic to suggest that our behavior and consciousness reflect the blending of all these centers in movement, in flux. The Siddhas tell us to glean true knowledge about them by meditating on them.

Union through "Ha" "tha" Yoga

The term *hatha* originates from two Sanskrit root sounds, "ha" and "tha." The sound "ha" represents the pranic flow of physical energy in the subtle solar channel, (*pingala nadi*), the positive masculine energy associated with physical functions and left brain function, which lies slightly to the right of the spinal cord, but in the vital body, emanating from the root adhara or muladhara. Nadis are not found in the physical body. The "tha" represents the flow of energy through the subtle lunar channel (*ida nadi*), the negative feminine current associated with consciousness and right brain function, emanating from muladhara and slightly to the left of the spinal cord. The root sounds, "ha" and "tha" signify the two opposing all pervasive forces of the universe, *prana* (upward moving force of consciousness) and *apana* (downward moving force of gravity). These are polar opposites, the positive and negative currents of energy, which manifest in human beings. Both these forms are pranic energy, which nourishes and sustains all life.

This animating force (bioplasm) is taken in with the breath. It is inhaled and exhaled with every breath. It is not oxygen; not a gas. The main objective in Hatha Yoga is to balance these two cosmic forces within the physical being. If *prana* and *apana* are brought in perfect balance in two of the main subtle nadis, *pingala* and *ida nadis* (found within the subtle spinal column), prana will merge with individualized consciousness into the third, more rarefied *sushumna nadi*, (coincident with the spinal cord). When the two behave as one, a new, spiritually potent ray of creative energy awakens (*kundalini shakti*). Individual consciousness expands and both hemispheres of the brain are enhanced. One begins to realize spiritual bliss as consciousness and energy become one, as mind and matter merge. Practice of the eighteen asana work directly on balancing the *ida* and *pingala nadis*. For the Siddhas, the term Hatha Yoga suggests regulation of breath or union of the two breaths, into the one.

The Siddhas tell us that the body is the mystic center, the sacred passageway to the Infinite Reality and that liberation is only available while incarnate in it. A practitioner of Kriya Hatha Yoga should undertake his/her practice with the aspiration of making the body a fit temple for the Lord, not merely figuratively, but literally. The body must be made a proper vessel prior to awakening the divine ray of *kundalini shakti*. *Kundalini* can be liken to a luminous snake, sleeping coiled three and half times around a *linga* (the self-originated phallus or a cosmic egg, the male seed of Being) at the root of the subtle spinal cord. The body and mind must be prepared to receive, channel and benevolently apply this divine potential power and consciousness. If the body and nervous system are not strong, when the coils of divine energy uncoil, the body will obstruct its manifestation or the energy will overwhelm the physical and mental systems. We can best keep the physical body healthy and the nervous system strong by practicing Hatha Yoga with aspiration for the Divine, and with devotion, as a means of worshipping this Divine *shakti* within.

The Seven Goals of Kriya Hatha Yoga

We practice Babaji's system of Hatha Yoga as a means of:
1) relaxation; **2)** physical well being and to bring homeostasis to the body, in terms of proper function of organs, establishing proper weight, and by nourishing tissues in body; **3)** purifying the physical body, mind and subtle energies, by eliminating toxins; **4)** bringing the body and mind to states of stillness and meditation; **5)** awakening our potential power and consciousness,

the *kundalini*, and of strengthening its magnetic *shakti* energy; **6)** developing detachment from external influences and developing equanimity; **7)** bringing about awareness of our divine origin, so the element of Self, imbibed in the body, can unveil itself as the Divine soul (Supreme consciousness). Such knowledge and power can be unveiled through the practice of postures faithfully, sincerely, regularly and with devotion.

1) Relaxation

The first goal of our practice of the 18 postures is relaxation. It is important that the asana are practiced slowly and with patience so as to gently stretch and strengthen the muscles, and to open and lubricate the joints. We learn to balance tension and relaxation. We balance strength and flexibility as we begin to utilize the deep muscles, not just the superficial ones. This increases muscular tone and length as it tranquilizes and soothes the nerves, inducing deep relaxation. An asana tones the physical body through its harmonious movements, while stimulating energy and increasing relaxation.

Yoga begins when there is no forcing or stress of any kind. This includes the subtle stress of frustration. When one forces oneself into a posture or experiences frustration, tension is created in the body and mind, blocking the flow of *prana*. The breath is the safe point of entry into the body. Right exertion occurs when the whole personality exerts itself and there is an intensity of concentration towards a definite goal, to stretch or bend in a new way. Only then will *prana* flow without obstruction.

The aim of Kriya Hatha Yoga is to find the right exertion to bring balance and relaxation to the body, breath and mind. By coordinating the breath with the physical movements, the heart rate is slowed, nerves are soothed and toned, the whole system is relaxed and the mind becomes passive. This synchronization brings more oxygen to the blood and releases more carbon dioxide and tension from the muscles. Stress signals (stretch reflexes), which are naturally sent to the brain when a muscle is stretched, are switched off, as the muscles are being stretched properly. The muscles relax and flexibility increases as disturbances in the body and the mind are eliminated. Deep and rhythmic breathing increases pranic energy, which develops muscle strength and endurance, and establishes steadiness and comfort in the asana.

By consciously observing and directing breath toward tightness in the musculature, muscles and joints are stretched safely. Each inhalation is naturally gathering universal life energy into the body, and this can be consciously directed to nourish blocked and tight areas in a stretch during exhalation. Each exhalation releases muscle fibers, allowing tension and tightness to relax. Making the exhalation longer than the inhalation will increase this "relaxation response."

With the use of a pranayama known as *ujjayi* (the victory or ocean-sounding) breath, one can create even deeper relaxation. *Ujjayi* breathing engages the whole personality and eliminates tensions uncovered as one moves deeper into postures. It stimulates the parasympathetic nervous system, which calms and relaxes. *Ujjayi* breathing is also known as the psychic breath, for it profoundly relaxes at the psychic level. It immediately withdraws the senses from the external world and influences the flow of *prana* in the subtle body channels, the *ida* and the *pingala*, which lie within the subtle spinal column. Awareness is built into the process.

Ujjayi uses long, slow and deep breathing through the nostrils (never through the mouth) with focused attention at the throat. A hissing sound is created by the slight constriction in the back of the throat, in the glottis. The tightening in the throat is similar to that required to gargle a liquid. This constriction narrows the air passage creating friction and so controls the flow of air. Both the inhalation and exhalation are lengthened. This muscular contraction produces a long "aaah" in the back of the throat, a sound similar to the ocean. Heard internally, it is soothing to the mind. Practice of this conscious breathing with your asana will deepen relaxation in your muscles. It will also ensure more life force is taken in and stored for normal use.

2) Well-being and homeostasis of the body

The second benefit of regular practice of Kriya Hatha Yoga is maintenance of one's health and homeostasis of the body. The asana and breath support the health of the tissues. The postures maintain tissue health by stimulating the supply of nourishment from the secretions of the endocrine glands and removing waste products, and by increasing healthy function of the nerve connections. The asana begin a systematic strengthening of the muscular system, nervous system, digestive and elimination systems, cardiovascular system, and the respiratory, reproductive and endocrine systems. Attention is focused on the joints in the body, to reduce stress and rigidity, and to increase lubrication. Healthy condition and flexibility of the joints can be restored in a relatively short time with regular practice. All the asana keep the spinal column supple, which creates the optimal flow of energy through the nerves, the organs and the glandular system. Kriya Hatha Yoga strengthens the bones, joints, muscles, connective tissues and organs, and reduces fatty tissue, all to keep the body youthful and in harmonious balance.

Regular practice of the asana and pranayama will alter brain chemistry and encourage emotional balance and harmony. Yoga is known to dampen dopamine activity in the basal ganglia. As a result, cravings and negative emotional states are inhibited. In addition, asana and pranayama trigger endorphins, which act as a natural pain reliever and grant a sense of well-being. The autonomic nervous system is stimulated through the shifting pressure changes within the internal organs. The actions of the sympathetic nervous system are slowed down, so the body is not flooded with stress hormones as quickly. Functioning of the parasympathetic system is improved. Blood pressure and heart rate are reduced and breathing becomes smooth, slow and deep, and all systems are able to normalize quickly. One is better able to relax, digest, sleep, and reflect. Once autonomic balance is achieved, so is emotional stability. The nervous system does not overreact to every incident. Blood pressure does not rise with every argument, nor does the heart pound because one is a bit late and afraid of missing a bus or plane.

The greatest benefits of Yoga come from tensing, relaxing and massaging of the tissues, while eliminating toxins and renewing and regulating vital life energy throughout the body. Just forcing oneself into a yoga posture carries little benefit. Health and vitality arise out of the release and increase of the flows of *prana*, the elemental life energy, generated in the pose. It is the *prana* that balances and nourishes the body, making it active, healthy and dynamic. An asana helps locate and massage the tight and rigid parts of the body where the *prana* is blocked or obstructed. Deep, rhythmic movement (*kriyas*) and relaxed, conscious breathing increases and directs *prana* through these areas, nourishing and healing them and increasing vitality. The practice of awareness also enables one to access *prana* at a more subtle level and direct its flow more effectively. It is when vital energy diminishes that the aging process begins. The individual becomes less active. The body becomes flabby due to loose muscles and bad postures. Fluids and tissues dry out and functional disorders of the organs and systems develop. By increasing and storing vital energy in the tissues and releasing toxins from them, regular Kriya Hatha Yoga maintains youthfulness throughout all the systems in the body.

This 18 posture series incorporates micro-movements, or *kriyas* in each asana and each static pose is followed by relaxation and a specific counter-pose. The *kriyas* loosen the body, deepen the pose and increase the circulation of oxygenated blood and lymph into tissues. The *kriyas* also help return venous blood, and stagnant lymph and waste products out of tissues. The relaxation and counter-poses assure that the toxins released from the tissues are moved to the organs of elimination and that there is a full circulation of oxygen, blood and lymph throughout the body. Energy is not allowed to become congested as it is moved along in the counterpose. Balance is established in the muscles and there is a consolidation of the increased magnetic energy.

Each posture is held for about two minutes, which is the time required to stretch connective tissue, gently massage internal organs, relax nerves and to experience release. Each posture is followed by thirty seconds (generally, not more than that) of total relaxation. This ensures that your yoga session will assimilate the new circulation and increase a sense of healing and well-being.

3) Purifying the physical body, mental body and subtle senses

Hatha Yoga is a stress-free system of cleansing and detoxification. The 18 postures is a concentrated intense practice of purification, which requires awareness, concentration and effort. The postures are so effective because they work holistically. They work directly on our anatomy and physiology and at the same time on our emotional, mental and spiritual dimensions. Through regular practice of Kriya Hatha Yoga many disorders and irregularities can be corrected.

Due to pollution in the air we breathe and additives in our food and stress in our lives, our bodies are laden with substances that cause health problems. The regular and proper practice of Hatha Yoga will remove toxins from all the cells of our body. As we move, twist, massage and move energy through our body our organ systems are purified. The practice of asana heats up the body as circulation increases. A quality of purification is heat. *Ujjayi* pranayama with the asana will increase the heating effect on the body.

Not only physical, but emotional purification can come naturally, as a result of regular and deep asana practice. Emotional memories and psychological pain becomes associated with various parts of our physical body and are often responsible for physical tightness, inflammation and pain. Any mental resistance, emotion or trauma stored within a tight area of the body can be released if the area is consciously stimulated and nourished with prana for a sufficient period of time.

The aim of our Kriya asana practice is not to achieve some quick success in performing difficult asana. The aim is to move comfortably into each asana and to hold it long enough to allow toxins to be released from the body and resistances to be released from the mind. Often one pushes into the final stage of an asana, but has to come out of it immediately. In performing each asana, reach into a position with enough tension to fully feel the stretch, but be comfortable enough to remain there. Comfort has to do with alignment and steadiness in the static posture. Proper breathing allows tension to be released and relaxed with each exhalation. Breathe slowly and deeply as the asana allows and remain concentrated on internal sensations of the stretch. Even deeply held psychological pain and trauma can be released from the cells of the body.

The Siddhas tell us that the soul comes into the physical body with three impurities or stains, known as *malas*. They are the *anava mala* (egoism), the *maya mala* (limiting appearances of life in the world) and the *karma mala* (present situations brought about by past actions). The Siddhas tell us that the spiritual dimension gives rise to all matter, and that all illness has its source in the spiritual body because of these three impurities. The spiritual body carries the above impurities and acquires more, rendering our mind and vital body subject to the two alternating forces of Nature known as *tamas guna* (attribute or qualities of inertia, laziness, darkness, doubt, fear, indifference and depression) and *rajas guna* (qualities of stimulation, agitation, pain, action, dispersion, desire, and anger). These impurities distort our view of the world and have huge repercussions throughout the mental, emotional, and physical bodies, which interpenetrate one another with their feelings and impulses. Therefore, any effort to overcome their dominance through a purification of the physical body must include also the vital-emotional, mental, intellectual and spiritual. Yoga asana, mudras, bandhas, mantras and devotion can be utilized effectively to encourage purification of all levels of our being. The goal of Yoga is to heal the whole being bringing about balance, buoyancy, knowledge or intellectual firmness, lucidity, contentment, and compassion, (all qualities of the *sattva guna*).

An intense concentrated practice must be undertaken for such holistic purification
Yogis know that by doing something repeatedly, exerting ourselves repeatedly, we can make anything a definite part of our mind and personality, positive or negative. An act of intense,

concentrated practice needs to be undertaken to strengthen, purify and discipline the mind and body. We can change a habit, or our nature, just by practicing the asana over and over again, until the practice is no longer an exertion. At that point, our practice has become transformative. We can burn through laziness and inertia and negligence and other mental conditioning. We can make change to negative habits of our mind (*samskaras*), which in turn determine much of our karma. In this way our asana practice can remove negative karma. Everything that we do, every act that we perform with our body, is planted in our mind. We strengthen our willpower every time we decide to do our yoga practice. Conversely, laziness is strengthened when we neglect it. Each and every act becomes a seed for self-empowerment in all areas of our life.

Take laziness, for example. Yoga can be used to eliminate laziness and to remove the karmic effect of laziness on the body, for instance, deposited fat and tightness. Either you work off the karma through the postures, or you pay for it by ending up with excess fat, illness or disease. Look at your own body. Where has your mind's actions and reactions deposited fat and/or tightness? You can work to remove them, as a form of karmic purification and to develop discipline, patience and perseverance. You expend some time and effort, perhaps even take on a little physical discomfort and pay off some karma and reap the benefits of having that karma removed. Yogis say do voluntarily and willingly those things you dislike doing; otherwise it will be obligatory. The Yogic saying is, "whatever you do not like to do, do it voluntarily."

4) Perfecting the posture by bringing the body and mind to a "still point"

The primary goal of our asana practice is "relaxation," however our objective takes us beyond the ordinary definition of the term. Our objective is immobility and mental stillness. We are reaching for the doorway to realizing our true spiritual Self with all of its potential power and consciousness. To reach this state of immobility, we must first rid ourselves of restlessness in the body. The experience of stillness is not due to a cessation of energy by inertia, but an increase of energy, an in-pouring and circulation of force. To master an asana is to be capable of holding great increases of energy and to endure its force with ease. The life force operates powerfully, but in a unifying movement on a tranquil and passive body, free from restlessness. A body accustomed to spiritual force becomes lighter, more buoyant, then filled with light and stills.

The perfection in asana is achieved by effortless effort and stillness. We can remain steady and stable in a pose for any length of time. We take our stretch deep inside the body. We use not only the superficial muscles, but also the deeper layers. The outside of the body is stretched firm and taut, yet inside the body feels softer, fluid and in-motion. The subtle channels are being stimulated to move more *prana* throughout them. Subsequently, we feel supported internally. This takes the burden off of the cardio-vascular and respiratory systems. Asana create more space in the body for the *prana*, offering an opportunity for healing and deepest relaxation.

Steadiness and stillness is achieved by holding *bandhas* (muscular locks) and *mudras* (gestures), during the postures. Bandhas bring about a natural balance of tension and relaxation and keep the central axis of the body aligned. They create greater tension in the muscles, supporting the sacro-iliac joint and lumbar spine and lift the ribcage. They enhance the energy flow. Postures can be held effortlessly for extended lengths of time. One may experience a new force of pulsating energy within.

Mudras help us contact the various flows of *prana* in the subtle body. A mudra is a switchboard of energy that sets up a specific circuit of energy that achieves mental and physical stillness. A mudra can be a physical or energetic vibration, or gesture or attitude, which helps us attain controlled psychic states. Without mudra we cannot experience meditation. Most often mudra is thought of as positions of the fingers, hands, face, eyes, or tongue. But, moreover, they are expressions or sensations of energy felt in the body. Mudras can also be created by a combination of asana and bandhas.

The **bandhas** create both safety and effectiveness in asana. A bandha is created when organs and muscles are contracted and controlled. The *mula bandha* squeezes the perineal muscles (pubo-coccygeal muscle, which goes from the pubic bone to the tail bone). *Uddiyana bandha* draws the navel inward and pulls the diaphragm upwards. *Jalandhara bandha* involves a forward flexion of the neck. *Maha bandha* engages all three contractions. These can be incorporated in postures quite naturally. Bandhas create a psycho-muscular energy contraction, which re-directs the flow of energy in the physical and subtle body. They work to support the physical body and to involve and align the physical with the mental and psychic bodies. The bandhas can unlock pranic and mental energy associated with the energy centers in the spine and brain.

Bandhas ensure that the whole system is working harmoniously, so less energy is required and more energy is stimulated. Physically, a bandha might involve squeezing the muscles of the perineum and/or contacting the abdomen and solar plexus. These contractions will have an effect on the nervous and circulatory systems. They balance the autonomic nervous system, reduce blood pressure, promote respiration and circulation and increase electromagnetic energy. They massage inner organs and stimulate the endocrine glands whose secretions bring about a sense of well-being. Bandhas can prevent the nervous system from being overloaded.

Use spinal breathing and still the body, mind and breath and awaken an expanded consciousness.

Because the energy of the breath (gross *prana*) and the energy of thoughts (subtle *prana*) are directly related, the breath is the bridge between the body and mind. By regulating the breath, you can slow down and even still your thoughts. You can begin to consciously take control of your mind through the use of spinal breathing and *ujjayi* pranayama. By synchronizing the inhalations and exhalations and directing your attention and energy along the spine (spinal breathing), or concentrating it at a specific point, you can move consciousness to a single point. This concentrated consciousness will take the mind into a natural state of meditation. As you inhale, visualize bringing energy up your spine. As you exhale visualize that energy expanding throughout your body. Use the *ujjayi* to keep your awareness turned inward and the *prana* will follow your attention. If awareness remains focused inward on the breath in the spine, the mind will begin to perceive these subtle energies.

5) Asana refine the body and moves us as human beings towards a more subtle energy existence

As we advance in our asana, we will experience the emergence of micro-vibrations within the body. When the asana become natural, easy and effortless, energy responds within. We might sense energy moving upward and downward, outward and inward or spiraling. We experience greater space in the body. We begin to feel hollow and empty, a shell filled with consciousness and energy. This energy is dynamic and feels transformative.

The practice of Kriya Hatha Yoga is a powerful means of awakening vital dynamism in the body. However, a posture can look perfect, yet not stimulate any pranic flow. Overly flexible people may get into even difficult poses easily, without any increase of energy. It is remiss to reduce asana to a gymnastic performance. Asana requires a balance of strength, flexibility and awareness of the energy flowing through it. An asana must increase force and direct *prana* in order to heal and regenerate tissues, and to expand consciousness. By concentrating on the spine or, better yet, on awakening vital energy in the spine, an asana can be corrected, perfected and mastered.

Kriya Hatha Yoga assists in the awakening of the *kundalini*. Although it is the *prana shakti* of the *kundalini* that keeps us going through the totality of all the experiences and activities of our lives, we are only using a fraction of its power and force. The Siddhas say this energy within each of us is *sat*, existence in matter and *chit*, consciousness. It is nothing less than a ray of the Divine, brilliant like ten thousand suns, a streak of lightening in the spine. Such is this power of *kundalini* that it not only moves everything, but can also still everything because the impulses of the *kundalini* are finer than any particle of matter discovered. As a result of *kundalini* awakening and rising in the *sushumna nadi*, the mind becomes concentrated, finely attuned to one single point in time, space and sequence. The whole body becomes firm.

The Siddhas say that when the *kundalini* becomes firm and not shaking, the whole body becomes firm, and becomes like the scriptural "flame in a room where there is no breeze." Everything becomes steady—voice, eyes, hearing, senses, words, mind, posture, standing, sitting - everything. Perfection of postures leads us to stillness of the mind. Perfecting an asana means that there is no more movement in us.

6) A means of developing detachment from external influences and developing equanimity

A student of Kriya Hatha Yoga should understand that ultimately it is the mind that disturbs the performance of his/her asana. The Siddhas suggest it is the mind's wrong decision-making which is the cause of all problems in a person's life. It is the mind that needs to be corrected and mastered. An asana practice can help discipline and correct the mind. As asana are mastered, changes should be seen not only in posture, flexibility or strength of body, but also in the way the mind works and in way the emotions respond to situations.

You can use asana to calm turbulent emotions. Holding your body in stillness concentrated on your breathing alters brain chemistry. As mentioned previously, Yoga reduces dopamine activity in the basal ganglia and as a result, cravings and negative emotional states are inhibited. In addition, asana with pranayama triggers endorphins, which relieve pain and stimulate a sense of well-being.

A disciplined and cheerful practice of asana can help tame emotions in general. Practiced regularly, Kriya Hatha Yoga will bring more peace and equanimity to your emotional life. You learn to observe and listen to what is happening in your body, instead of just reacting to disturbances. You naturally begin to separate part of your consciousness, so that you can watch sensations, thoughts and emotions as they arise within you. You learn to see them as somehow separate from who you are.

Learning to be the observer of what you are thinking, feeling or doing creates the time and space required to discriminate and detach. You become more mentally and emotionally disciplined. You find that you are not so easily distracted by discomfort in the body, heat or cold, or pain or pleasure, likes or dislikes, craving or satisfaction, or praise and blame. Even asana practice offers you a wonderful opportunity to conquer the pairs of opposites.

To master an asana, the body must be in perfect balance. The body is still and at ease and the mind is fixed at one point. To be a master of Yoga, the mind is at ease and equipoise is maintained in all aspects of life. Mastery of a posture can lead to mastery of life, if your practice has developed your discipline and willpower on all levels of your being. This is the great teaching of the Siddhas: "the amount of happiness in life is proportional to one's discipline."

7) A means of bringing about awareness of our divine and infinite origin

Mastering asana involves relaxing effort and attuning the mind in the expansive qualities of the infinite, pure sensation, pure vibration. The immortal Siddhas say that the yogi's consciousness is the entire life force, which exists in the whole universe, and that the realized yogi is plugged into and thinks, speaks, acts and lives through the unlimited and infinite life force existing in the infinite universe.

But what about the rest of us? Can we mere mortals experience the Infinite? Yes. First, even through our practice of Kriya Hatha Yoga we can develop a perception of ourselves as "beings of energy." We can realize that the physical body is made up of energy and empty space and that what we are is more energy than matter. We are *That*, which has taken possession of an inert form and made it come alive. Our living being is pure energy.

Second, we can experience the Infinite by dedicating our practice as a ritual of worship (kriya) and by making the intention to have a vision of the Self within. The *rishis* (yogis) declare that a person must only master one pose, maintaining it for about three hours, keeping the mind in meditation on an infinite object to reach a stage of "*asana siddhi*," of *Samadhi*, of cognitive absorption.

Even before you can remain motionless for three hours in a pose, you can have an experience of the Infinite Space. You simply need to choose to remain aware in your practice.

On a physical level, notice the position of your spine. Keep your spine straight and your abdominal muscles tightened, your pelvic floor lifted, and your breath deep and relaxed, increasing the gross *prana*. Relax into *ujjayi* breathing. Observe what is happening in your inner body and direct subtle *prana* into any tightness. Keep your mind as silent and passive as possible. Allow your awareness to be drawn to one point and concentrate there. Experiencing the silencing of the senses, the mind quieting, the breath becoming subtle, you can rest in beingness. With your mind concentrated at one point, observe the flow of *prana*, and the breath which begins and ends, and begins again. Become aware of what is aware; that is, become aware of the steady feeling of Presence and become more and more aligned with your true nature.

Chapter 3
The 18 Posture Series

Practicing the Postures

Stand up straight with your feet hip distance apart. Bring your heels in, letting them touch. Your feet are separated, in a thirty degree angle. Spread your toes, to better balance your weight. The little toe on each foot should touch the ground. Press down gently through the heel and the ball of both feet. This push against the ground is a push against the effects of gravity. Your body will respond by feeling lighter as your muscular energy rises. Your legs are straight, but the knees are not locked. There is a sense of relaxation through the legs. Tighten your thighs; both your hamstrings and quadriceps contract. Tighten your pelvic floor. You do this by squeezing the muscles that you would use to stop urination. Pull your navel center in, so that the lower abdominal muscles are contracted. These two contractions support your lower back and help to straighten your spine.

Open your shoulders, bringing your shoulder blades down. Allow your arms to fall naturally along side of your body. Your chest is open. Your ribcage lifts upward, so it is off of your belly. Look straight ahead. Imagine a gentle lifting from the crown of your head. Bring your hands together in prayer position (*vanekom mudra*) at the center of your chest. Your thumbs press against your sternum.

Inhale deeply and chant the mula mantra, *Om Kriya Babaji Nama Aum*. Chanting the mula mantra is a natural tranquilizer. It calms and centers the mind. It creates an immediate mind-body connection, relaxing the body, quieting the nervous system and causing blood pressure and the heart rate to drop.

The Mula Mantra Defined

Om – the primordial sound of the universe, embedded in your nervous system. It is said that chanting 'O' strengthens the body, chanting 'm' strengthens the cerebrum. **Kriya** – one of the three great energies of the universe: *kriya shakti, jnana shakti and icchi shakti. Kriyashakti* is the energy of action, *jnanashakti* is the energy of wisdom and *icchishakti*, the energy of will or intention. "**Babaji**" – Divine Father. Babaji is the living source and fountainhead of Kriya

Yoga; it is truly your own highest Self. **Nama** – "salutations," or, "my name is." **Aum** – the vibration resonating within yourself. This mantra is a "call" to your own highest Self; it is a call for Grace and Awareness to be present in your actions.

The 1st Asana – *Kriya Asana Vanekom*, **The Saluation Pose**

This is a **Posture of Salutation** to the Self. This first pose aligns and integrates all five bodies in the practice. The Tamil Siddhas have told us that "the human body is the mystic center, the sacred passage to the ultimate reality and that liberation is available only within it." Therefore, to meditate on the Self, to worship the Self, begins the practice of Yoga. This first posture, *Kriya Asanan Vanekom* orients the entire being to the worship of the Divine and to the recognition that the body is a "temple" worthy of Infinite care.

Salutation Pose is an "offering." We are "offering" our head to the Guru, your supreme source of guidance and wisdom, whose center is in the *sahasrara*, the crown chakra. We are "offering" our separate will to Divine Will. With our head towards the ground and our feet upwards, and our hands and palms together, reaching above the head we attempt to enter the zone of the Guru, the zone of Love. The pose should be practiced with Love. This pose is symbolic of *Samadhi*. In this posture it is possible for the *prana vayu* to settle within the head, which means that there is an equal pressure from head to foot and we can rest in a state of utter tranquility.

◆ Knee down with your knees together, your arms by your side. The physical body aligns with the physical posturing of kneeling. Tighten the pelvic floor, by squeezing the muscles of the perineum and pull the navel center in toward the spine.

◆ Bring your chin to your chest and place the crown of your head to the floor about a hand length away from your knees.

◆ Bring both hands in front of the head with palms together.

◆ Lift your feet and rock forward, balancing on the knees, the forearms and the crown of your head. There should be no pressure on your elbows.

◆ The vital body and mental body will align as you **roll your eyes upward** concentrating on the inside of the skull at the crown of your head **and breathe** into that point.

◆ The intellectual body aligns as you **chant the mantra**, *Om Kri ya Ba ba ji Na ma A u m*

◆ The spiritual body completes the alignment with your aspiration for grace and awareness to descend. Continue to hold the pose, meditating on the point between the brows or at the crown of the head, the home of All-pervading Divine Consciousness, for one to three minutes.

◆ Release your legs down, and sit back between your heels. Your right big toe placed over your left big toe. Take a moment to absorb the experience before coming up to a standing pose.

◆ Bring your heels together with your feet apart. Your hands are at your chest in prayer pose. Open your shoulders, bringing your shoulder blades downward. The chin drops, the eyes are forward, the crown of your head lifts. Notice the sense of calmness and lightness throughout the body.

Kriya Asana directly stimulates all the nerves of the head and the pituitary and pineal glands, whose secretions, including endorphins, invigorate the entire glandular system. It stretches and relaxes the whole spine, stretching all the movable vertebra in the spine. The cervical vertebra and windpipe is made more elastic. Circulation is improved in the spine and brain. The eyes are relaxed and refreshed. The whole body is refreshed. It is useful for people with low blood pressure. Salutation pose stimulates the brow (*ajna*) and crown chakra (*sahasrara*), if eyes are turned upward and concentration remains focused for 1-3 minutes. It can stimulate a more peaceful temperament.

The 2nd Asana – *Kriya Surya Namaskar*, **Salutation to the Sun**

The Sun is also worthy of our salutation. It sends us vital energy in the form of luminous light. The earth would not be held in place were it not for the sun, which holds it secured on its axis. The sun is the most obvious symbol of the Light of Consciousness that we can see, as its energy is the same energy that moves through us, animating us.

Try as often as possible to practice this salutation series outside in the early morning sunlight before nine in the morning. It is said that the sun's white light is absorbed within the subtle body, refracted into the seven colors and directed to specific parts of the body for health and healing. Sunlight strengthens one's health and aura. The aura repels and attracts according to one's particular vibration. Building and magnifying the aura is as important as is strengthening and purifying the body and mind.

The postures of the sun salutation stretch, warm and tone the body by stimulating the functioning of various systems in the body, the muscular, respiratory, digestive, circulatory, nervous, endocrine and sensory systems. In addition, when the mantra, OM KRIYA BABAJI NAMA AUM, is chanted, minute vibrations are generated that have a subtle effect of purification on all the vital organs, especially the cerebrum, heart and stomach. The chant arouses subtle senses through the harmony it encourages within the body. It stimulates energy centers and strengthens the aura. It creates a relaxation response and can cause a measurable drop in blood pressure and heart rate. The breath deepens with the mantra, muscles relax and brain activity changes.

Take time as you move through the various positions of the sun salutation. Close your eyes, and drench yourself in the breath and the light of consciousness. When you practice outside in the sun, you receive the additional benefits of the circulation of the sun's rays.

****

Move slowly through each pose in the series, holding each for one or more breaths. Vibrate the chakras by chanting aloud the mantra, Om Kriya Babaji Nama Aum,

- ◆ Raise your arms **above your head,** palms touching -- **Chant** *Om Kriya Babaji Nama Aum.*
- ◆ Take your palms to your **forehead center** -- **Chant** *Om Kriya Babaji Nama Aum.*
- ◆ Take your palms to your **throat center** -- **Chant** *Om Kriya Babaji Nama Aum.*
- ◆ To your **heart center** -- **Chant** *Om Kriya Babaji Nama Aum.*
- ◆ To your **navel center** -- **Chant** *Om Kriya Babaji Nama Aum.*
- ◆ Come onto your **knees,** bring your **hands together on top of your head** -- **Chant** *Om Kriya Babaji Nama Aum.*
- ◆ **Salutation Pose** - Bring your head to the floor about a hand's length from your knees. Your arms are above your head, palms together. Lift your legs, balancing on the knees, forearms and crown of the head. Focus your concentration on the inside of the skull at

the crown of the head -- **Chant** *Om Kriya Babaji Nama Aum.*

Move into **Equestrian Pose**: Slide your right knee forward and left leg back. Press down in your hands, placed by the knees. Relax the shoulders back, lift your heart, and expand your chest. Extend your neck, lift the chin. Focus your concentration between the brows. **Chant** *Om Kriya Babaji Nama Aum.*

Moving into **Mountain Pose**: Slide your right knee back. Press your hands and toes into the floor, lift your buttocks up, shift your pelvis back and through the legs. Your head is between your arms. Your body forms a triangle with the floor. Drop your chin to your chest. Look back at your knees. Focus concentration on your throat chakra. **Chant** *Om Kriya Babaji Nama Aum.*

Move into **Cobra**: Release the right leg back to the floor, and your left leg. Lower your hips down. Your legs are together or hip distance apart. The tops of the feet are on the floor. Tighten your pelvic floor, tightening the muscles as you would to stop urination. Pull your navel center in. Bring your arms to the level of your shoulder. Elbows are close to the body. Roll your shoulders backward; your shoulder blades move downward. Push your chest forward and lift up into cobra. Begin to use the arm muscles as you raise the torso up even further to arch the spine. Take your time. Extend the neck, your face moves upward. Focus concentration where you feel the pressure at the sacrum. Inhale and chant the mantra. **Chant** *Om Kriya Babaji Nama Aum.*

Moving into **8-point salutation**: Press your toes into the floor, lower the chest, and lift the pelvis. 8-points touch - 2 toes, 2 knees, 2 hands, chest and chin. Keep your buttocks and stomach lifted. There is a natural *uddiyana bandha* (the abdomen is drawn back and up, and the diaphragm is pulled under the ribs; the navel is pulled toward the back of the body). The spine is arched. Focus at the solar plexus, *manipura chakra.* Inhale and chant. **Chant** *Om Kriya Babaji Nama Aum.*

Now **reverse** back into **Cobra**. Bring the top of your feet back to the floor, lowering the pubis back down and push the chest forward as you lengthen the spine and again lift upwards. The spine is arching and the head is facing up in Cobra. Focus again at the sacrum on *swadhisthana chakra* and **chant** *Om Kriya Babaji Nama Aum.*

Turn your toes into the floor and come up onto your hands and knees. Shift your weight backwards and lift your hips up, straightening your arms, and legs. Come back into **Mountain Pose**. Press into your palms but shift your pelvis back and through your legs. Drop your head to your chin and focus on *vishuddhi chakra.* Inhale and **chant** *Om Kriya Babaji Nama Aum.* Bring the outside edge of your feet towards the floor, stretching the whole backside of your body.

Come up on your toes and bring your **left knee forward on the floor** between the hands and extend your right leg back. Relax the shoulders back and down and lift your chest, forming

Equestrian Pose again. Feel the expansion at the heart. Lift the chin, lengthening the neck. Free up the energy in the spine, and focus between the brows at *ajna chakra*. Breathe in and out from that point. **Chant** *Om Kriya Babaji Nama Aum.*

Bring your **left knee back** to your **right** and **bring your palms together**. Bring your head to the floor about a hand's length from your knees into **Salutation Pose**. Lift your legs, balancing on the knees, forearms and crown of the head. Focus your concentration on the inside of the skull at the crown of the head. **Chant** *Om Kriya Babaji Nama Aum.*

Kneel up, bringing your hands together on top of your head. **Chant** *Om Kriya Babaji Nama Aum.* Visualize the descent of grace.

Stand up and bring your palms together **at the manipura chakra (navel center)**. **Chant** *Om Kriya Babaji Nama Aum.*

Bring your hands at a**nahata chakra (heart center)**. **Chant** *Om Kriya Babaji Nama Aum.*
And now at the **vishuddhi chakra (throat center)**. **Chant** *Om Kriya Babaji Nama Aum.*
And now at the **ajna chakra, or third eye (between the eyebrows)**. **Chant** *Om Kriya Babaji Nama Aum.*
And finally at the **sahasrara chakra (crown center, above your head)**. **Chant** *Om Kriya Babaji Nama Aum.*
Turn in a clockwise direction, chanting the **Song of Sunworship**.

The Song of the Science of Sunworship pays homage to Supreme Consciousness in the form of the Divine Light of the Sun and in all the various forms of light in our universe, and to all the important principles and practices of Kriya Yoga. Through it, we express our aspiration for the Lord and for "Grace," that blessing, which is undeserved, unexpected and bestowed upon us. Finally, we pay homage to the Gurus in this tradition: Babaji (Holy Father), *Mataji* (Holy Mother) and *Amman* (Brother).

Turn in a clockwise direction, turning a quarter of a turn, as you chant each line aloud. Chant with humility and gratitude, and envision grace descending through the top of the head like rays or raindrops. Just as in India, you might circumambulate a temple to magnetize your body and receive grace, so too you turn your body around, circumambulating your own Divine Temple. The clockwise movement itself will magnetize your aura. Your aura will become a blessing to you and to all who come in contact with you.

Deepam Jyoti Parabrahman	Waving and worshipping with the Supreme Grace Light
Deepam Sarvam Tamobagam	I aspire for Grace
Deepanay Sathyathey Sarvam	Through Truth may all be done
Nyarua Deepam Namosthuthey	Salutations to the Sun
Kaalai Deepam Namosthuthey	Salutations to the light in the morning
Ucchi Deepam Namosthuthey	To the mid-daylight
Santhyaa Deepam Namosthuthey	To light of the evening
Nisi Deepam Namosthuthey	The light that shines in dark night
Anbu Deepam Namosthuthey	To Divine Love
Ahimsa Deepam Namosthuthey	To Non-violence
Asana Deepam Namosthuthey	To postures of relaxation
Prana Deepam Namosthuthey	To mastery of breathing
Dhyana Deepam Namosthuthey	To mastery of the mind
Jnana Deepam Namosthuthey	To Supreme Self-knowledge
Mantra Deepam Namosthuthey	To the sacred syllables
Bhakti Deepam Namosthuthey	To love and devotion of the Divine
Babaji Deepam Namosthuthey	To Babaji, Divine Father
Annai Deepam Namosthuthey	To Mataji, Divine Mother
Amman Deepam Namosthuthey	To Amman, Divine brother *(Swami Pranabananda)*
Yoga Deepam Namosthuthey	To the Scientific Art of perfect God-Truth-Union

Bring your hands to your heart. Roll your shoulders open, bringing your shoulder blades down. Press down through the heel and ball of each foot, spread your toes. Breathe in deeply. Breathe out fully. Let go into the sensations of energy flowing in your body. Notice the quality of your breath and how you feel. Your body is warm and supple, your breath relaxed, your mind calm and passive.

****

The 3rd Asana - *Sarvangasana*, The Shoulder Stand

Sarvangasana or Shoulder Stand is considered one of the most important of all asanas. It continues to warm up the body. We move into this powerful inversion to unblock energy by placing the body under pressure and reversing its normal functioning. It draws the mind into the body. The mind focuses automatically due to the pressure on the body. Awareness is increased. Inversions revitalize the whole system and begin a process of cleansing at the deepest levels. As the physical pressure is released the body comes into balance as tension stored in the upper back, shoulders and neck are relaxed. Tremendous energy can be unleashed at the area of the throat. Shoulder Stand can even grant psychic relief from some of the burden egoism places on the mind.

Virtually every system of the body benefits: circulatory, digestive, respiratory, lymphatic and the autonomic nervous systems. Shoulder Stand rejuvenates every organ, alleviates fatigue in the legs and feet, nourishes the cells in the face, brings calm, and is good for sound sleep. By reversing the flow of gravity, every muscle is flushed with blood. Circulation is increased in all the major glands and organs, including pituitary, pineal glands, heart, lungs, kidneys, liver, spleen, ovaries and uterus. Being inverted strengthens the diaphragm, which results in deeper breathing. It clears the mind and nourishes the brain, and strengthens and calms the nervous system, by stimulating the thyroid and parathyroid glands, which regulate metabolism. The stretch in the neck stimulates the parasympathetic nerve stretch receptors to lower both blood pressure and pulse rate. This asana is used therapeutically for asthma, dyspepsia, constipation, hernia and for degeneration of the testes or ovaries.

Shoulder Stand is often referred to as "all members pose," because it requires muscular effort throughout the entire body. The whole body is actively helping the upper extremities support the pose. It requires a sense of strength and balance. If the pelvic floor is lifted (squeezing the perinea muscles, as in *mulabandha*) and the navel center tightened and pulled in toward the spine it will give support to the sacral and lumbar regions and lengthen the spine. The cervical region should be warmed and strengthened through conscious relaxation and neck flexion and extension exercises, prior to going up into the inversion. *Ujjayi* breathing and elongating the exhalation will internally support the position of the body and increase the cleansing effects. Shoulder Stand increases overall awareness, as it relaxes and revitalizes the body.

****

Lay down on your back with your head, neck and spine in alignment. Your arms are placed along your body with palms facing downward. Bend your knees and fold your legs in over your chest. We first loosen up the joints in the feet to eliminate energy blockages and aid the return of stagnant lymph and venous blood. Open and stretch your toes. Wiggle them for at least thirty seconds. Flex your feet forward and backward for the same amount of time. Be aware of the physical movement, the interrelation between the joints and the bones, ligaments and muscles, and fascia, how every movement is in relation to other parts of the body. Notice that this movement can help relax your neck muscles. Release your head slowly from side to side. Stretch into any tension you might encounter. Rotate both your ankles clockwise and then counter clockwise. These small movements will help to slow brain waves and enhance relaxation. Stretching your feet can relieve tiredness and cramps in the body and will benefit those with poor circulation. Breathe deeply. Begin spinal breathing. Imagine your breath traveling up from the base of your spine with each inhalation and expanding throughout the body with each exhalation.

Next, squeeze your pelvic floor muscles (as in *mulabandha*), and contract your lower abdominal muscles (pull the navel inward). This will give support to your sacral and lumbar spine. Lengthen your neck. Press down into your hands and roll up from the sacrum, bringing your knees to rest on your forehead.

Take your hands to your lower back, waist height, to support your back. Bring your upper arms and elbows parallel to each other and let your hands support the torso from the back. Shift your shoulder blades down toward your waist. Bring your elbows close, in order to bring the shoulders close. This creates a triangle between the back of the head and the shoulders to better protect your neck and shifts the weight away from the neck and onto the shoulders. The neck does not touch the floor in this position.

Keep your pelvic floor muscles squeezed and lower abdominal muscles tightened. Press down through the back of your head and lift your legs upward effortlessly. Tighten the deep muscles of your back and contract your hip flexors. Breathe a line of energy upward along the spine and inner thighs. Breathe deeply. Press your pelvis forward. Keep the legs active. Don't flex your feet. You can relax them or you can dorsi-flex the toes, flexing them in the direction of your head.

As you move into the classic Shoulder Stand the spine will straighten and the sternum will move toward the chin to create a chin lock (*jalandhara bandha*). Your legs will come to vertical so the pelvis is directly above the shoulders. When the pelvis is directly above the shoulders the weight of the body comes directly down onto the shoulders and not into the neck. The pelvic diaphragm remains contracted, abdominal muscles and hip flexors tightened and the whole body is actively aiding the upper extremities.

When you have a full version of the Shoulder Stand, the pressure from the entire body will be pushing against the chin. The head and neck are immobile. This can release tension and blocked energy and revitalize the body, but it requires rhythmic breathing and relaxation in both body and mind.

Smooth rhythmical breathing is integral to this posture. Notice that with your chest pressed up against your chin you have a natural *ujjayi* breath. The "ocean sounding breath" is created due to friction created by the breath flowing through the restricted air passage. It will give additional support to the pose. Lengthen the exhalation as you can to increase the cleansing properties of this pose. Gaze at your feet and hold concentration there, or close your eyes and focus on the throat chakra (*vishuddhi*). Notice how the mind calms.

Slowly lower your knees to your forehead. Bring your hands to the floor and roll your spine vertebra by vertebra to the floor. When your buttocks touches the floor, extend your legs upwards and hold for several breaths.

Make sure your abdominal and pelvic floor muscles are tightly contracted as you lower your legs as slowly as possible. If your abdominal and/or back muscles feel strain, just bend your knees and bring your feet to the floor.

Relax onto your back in *shavasana* (corpse pose). Allow your shoulders, arms and hands, legs and feet to roll outward, open. Turn your palms upward. If you keep your arms and legs close to the body, you will hold onto tension.

Notice the quality of your breath. You may feel some tingling sensations of energy in the extremities, throat and shoulders or in the back where there has been a concentration of circulation during the pose. The relaxation phase assimilates this energy. Each asana is a mind-body diagram, which circulates energy throughout the body. The asana moves blood, lymph, *prana* and waste products. During the relaxation stage the circulatory system carries away the waste products that have been released into it in the pose. It carries them away to the organs of elimination such as the skin, the lungs and the colon, and so removes the source of fatigue and ultimately the source of toxins. We must remain in relaxation for no less than thirty seconds in order to assimilate this exchange. Be aware of any inner sensations of discomfort, consciously releasing them with an exhalation.

To tone all the muscles and stretch the spine, reach your arms above your head and stretch.

Point and flex your toes. Come up, reaching for your toes on an exhalation. To protect your back, tighten your abdominal and pelvic floor muscles and bring your chin to your chest. It is important to tone up the muscles in this way, after relaxing them in *shavasana*.

Caution: This inversion is counterindicated during menses. People with high blood pressure, glucoma or an enlarged thyroid should discuss the therapeutic benefits and complications of doing this posture, with a health professional

The 4th Asana - *Meenasana*, or *Matsyasana*, Fish Pose, (counterpose)

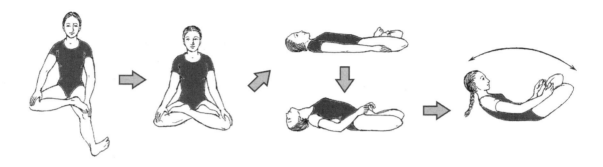

Matsyasana or **Fish Pose** is said to have been named for the great Siddha Macchamuni or Matsyendranath. The Siddhas say that one of the purposes of Hatha Yoga is to uncover habitual tendencies of the unconscious mind (*samskaras*), which influence the physical. Asana builds a bridge between the body and the deepest recesses of the mind. *Meenasana, Fish Pose*, is an asana that invites impressions, which have taken root in the subconscious, to be released. With the chest lifted, the heart is open and free to release what the mind might otherwise censor. Remaining in the pose for extended lengths of time can open one to a fuller vision of what is there. In addition, this pose is said to grant spiritual nourishment by opening the spiritual heart and intuition.

Meenasana is the counter-pose to Shoulder Stand. They should be practiced together because one flexes the neck in the opposite direction to the position held in the previous pose. This counter-stretch releases residual tension and energy in the neck and shoulders. This opposite stretching massages the muscles in a continuous circular pattern, which prevents congestion of blood and energy. The Fish Pose increases blood circulation and tones the nerves and tissues and muscles of the neck and shoulders. These areas receive optimum nutrition and conduct more efficient maintenance and repair. Shoulder stand followed by fish pose increases circulation in the thyroid and parathyroid glands, aiding thyroid function and stabilizing metabolism. The internal secretions of the parathyroid glands are very important in the health and development of body and mind. The secretions assist the absorption and assimilation of calcium in the body.

With Fish Pose, the cervical and thoracic vertebral column receives immense benefits. The positioning of the head shortens the space between the posterior portions of the cervical vertebra, so move into the pose slowly. This position lowers blood pressure as it stimulates stretch receptors in the neck. These receptors send signals to the central nervous system in response to the steady blood pressure and the rate of change of blood pressures within the blood vessels in the neck. The stretch in the throat has a toning affect on the larynx. This increases circulation and also benefits the cranial nerves in the base of the skull by relieving stress and pressure from the vascular system of the brain. The total result is a relaxation of the central nervous system.

The Fish Pose lifts the chest, arching the back, so that the weight of the body rests at the crown of the head. This encourages deep thoracic breathing. It will increase the volume of air in the lungs and is often used in the treatment for asthma and bronchial conditions. The heart is well-massaged and all the glands receive a good supply of blood. Digestive power increases in the pose. Pelvic congestion is relieved in ovaries and uterus. This pose also stimulates internal "breathing" and circulation of *prana* in the spinal cord.

Fish Pose is an asana that benefits in particular those who sit with a collapsed posture sitting in front of a computer screen all day. It can help to manage the stress of work, life and family responsibilities. The Fish Pose can make changes in the personality. Because it stimulates the secretion of endorphins directly from the glands in the brain, it can remedy bouts of sadness, depression or anxiety.

Do each stage of the pose slowly and with attention and awareness on the breath. Do the pose with interest and willingness. Do not use force or allow yourself to become frustrated. Investigate each position or stage and move into it to the fullest extent that your body will allow you to, each day. Each day your body will be in a different condition, so pay attention to how it feels. Do not force it. Respect your limitations. Remain at one stage until your body is comfortable and your breath is flowing easily. If a stage is uncomfortable, you might want to examine what is uncomfortable about it and adjust the pose and breathe into the discomfort. Always back out of what is painful. However, do bend into what is tight, using the breath to open the way. Aim for a feeling of effortlessness and poise at each stage, before you move on. When you feel no need to move out of a position, no desire to move on, you have discovered a place of stillness in both body and mind, so stay there and breathe deeply. Observe sensations and breathe out whatever arises. Do not think. Simply feel the sensations present. Emotions may be released, with or without memory. Insights will arise.

****

Begin *meenasana* by first loosening up the hip joints, to prepare for the full lotus. Remember, a full lotus is something to work towards, but should never be forced.

Sit on your sitting bones (ischial tuberosity) and lengthen your spine. Bring the soles of your feet together and your heels as close to your body as is comfortable. Place your hands on your knees and gently flutter the knees toward the floor for 45 seconds. Take hold of your feet.

Press your elbows against your inner thighs. Lengthen your spine with your inhalation and release forward on exhalation. Keep your chin up and your back flat. Release downward only on exhalations. Relax into the stretch in the hips for 90 seconds, breathing long and deep. This will increase circulation in your pelvic organs. The nerves become strong as the electromagnetic power of the body increases. Release back up.

Bend your left knee and place your left foot into the crook of your right arm. Keep your foot flexed to better stabilize the knee and keep your back straight. Wrap both arms around the leg, cradling it. Interlace your fingers and rock the leg from one side to the other side, opening your hip joints for 30 seconds. Release the grip of your hands and just circle the left bent leg so the left hip joint releases a bit more. Move your leg clockwise and counterclockwise, using large circles. If you feel tightness in the hip or knee, massage or rapidly rub the tight areas.

Bring your left foot as far over and as far up on your right thigh as is comfortable. Make sure that your left ankle is being supported on your right thigh. Hold onto your left foot with your right hand and with the left hand lift and lower your left knee. Inhale as you take the knee up and exhale as you bring it down toward the floor. Don't press the knee to the floor if you experience any tension in the knee cap, just bring it to horizontal position. When you feel a release in the left hip, lower and release the leg. Vigorously pat out any tension on both sides of the leg.

Bend your right knee, and flexing your right foot place it into the crook of the left elbow. Cradle your leg with both arms and rock the leg from side to side. You can deepen the stretch by pressing your leg toward your chest and your chest toward the leg. Continue to rock and open the right hip. Make certain that your back is straight not rounded. Release the tight grip and just circle the leg so the hip joint releases more. Move the leg in both directions, using large circles. Again with this leg, take time to massage or rapidly rub areas of tension in the hip, the knee or the ankle.

Bring your right foot as far over and as far up on your left thigh as comfortable. Make sure that you are not putting pressure on your ankle. The right ankle should be supported by your thigh. Hold onto your right foot with your left hand and with the right hand lift and lower your right knee. Inhale as you take the knee up and exhale as you bring it down toward the floor. Don't force the knee all the way to the floor. Gently press the knee down. If you experience any tension in the knee cap, just lift the knee upward, returning it only to the horizontal position. Release the leg, massage and pat out any tension on both sides of the leg.

The Lotus: Sitting on your sitting bones, and with your spine straight, move into a full lotus. *Take hold of your left shin and ankle from underneath your left leg, so you rotate the shin and thigh outward (don't grab your foot above your leg). Keeping your foot flexed, glide your left foot as high and as far over on top of your right thigh as you comfortably can so that your left ankle is supported on your right thigh. If the ankle bends so that the sole of your foot faces up at you, the ankle is weakened and there is an excessive pull on the ligaments and cartilage of the knee. Bend your right knee, flex the right foot, take your right ankle and shin from underneath and ease your right leg on top of your left. Relax your feet. If you don't experience comfort and stability in this posture, release your right leg and cross it under you. If you experience pain in the left leg, sit in sukasana, easy pose (both legs crossed under you).

First stage: Take hold of your big toes, open your shoulders and bring your shoulder blades down. Lengthen your spine and expand your chest and release forward, with an exhalation. Try to keep your spine lengthened. Lengthen, rather than round your lumbar spine. Begin little kriyas, micro-movements, easing your torso forward, as your hips open. Bring your forehead toward the floor. Relax with the breath to allow additional opening in the hips. Release back up.

Second stage: Squeeze your pelvic muscles and contract your abdominals to protect your spine, drop your chin to your chest. Your hands are still holding your toes. Take a deep breath and roll backwards, bringing your knees upward as your back rolls onto the floor. Try to ease your legs toward the floor in front of you. Use the kriyas, pulsing gently. If you can, drop your legs all the way to the floor and breathe into the increasing stretch in your lower back.

Third stage: To move into the Fish Pose, bring your elbows and forearms on the floor along side your body. Slip your fingers under your upper thighs and sit up. Your sitting bones should aim down towards the floor and the pubic bones aim forward as you lift your chest and lengthen your neck. Lift your chin. Look upward. Inhale deeply, drawing breath up the spine. Slowly create a deeper arch in your spine, by lifting at your heart. This will arch your thoracic vertebra and give some release in your lumbar vertebra. Lower the top of your head to the floor (if you cannot bring the top of the head to the floor, simply lift the chin and look upward, releasing the head backward and continue to support yourself with your forearms).

If your head is well positioned and supported by the floor and your back and neck muscles feel strong, gently release the support of the arms. Place your hands on your thighs or reach again for your toes.

Adjust the position of your head to attain the maximum comfortable arch in the spine. Feel the expansion through your chest. Your breath will slow and deepen. The positioning of the vertebrae of the neck and upper portion of the back will encourage powerful breathing and stimulate blood flow into the spine. The entire front of the body is stretched, the abdomen and diaphragm, the chest, intercostals and pectoral muscles are expanded and the rib cage opened. Keep your pelvic floor held tightly, and your navel center contracted. Continue spinal breathing. Visualize energy rising in the spine as you inhale and feel it expand through the chest, as you exhale.

Bring the epicenter of your awareness to the area of the heart or throat. You may feel energy flowing in your chest, or experience a sense of lightness, buoyancy, and sense of well-being. The breath is natural. The breath may become more and more subtle as you begin to hold the pose effortlessly. Remain content, your body still, your mind calm, for about two minutes. Note: Always come out of a pose if you experience discomfort.

Last stage: Slip your forearms back down to the floor and use their support to carefully release the back of your head and neck to the floor. Bring your crossed legs upward and grasp your toes. Contract your pelvic floor and abdominal muscles again, and bring your chin into your chest as you roll on the spine forward and backward. Exhaling, roll forward, bringing your forehead toward the floor. Then, inhale and roll backwards onto your shoulders (not your neck). Continue like this, rolling forward exhaling and backwards inhaling. The movement and your breathing should be connected and smooth. This rolling movement creates more space between the vertebra and allows an increase of energy to flow in the spine and out through the capillaries into the rest of the body.

Roll back to a sitting position and bring your hands to rest at your knees. Sit still, observe and enjoy the calm flow of energy throughout body and mind.

Stretch your legs out. Massage any tension from your knees and briskly rub or pat both sides of your legs.

Relax onto your back in *shavasana*. Relax your shoulders and arms, so that they drop away from your body. Your palms roll upward. Spread your legs apart and let your feet roll open. Release your head and neck from side to side to release any blocked energy.

Notice the quality of your breath and release any discomfort in your body or mind with your exhalations. Breathe out whatever arises. There is no need to think about or examine anything. There is no need to label anything. Simply feel whatever sensation is present and let go.

Yoga says, whatever happens in the body is a reflection of what has already happened in the mind, and conversely, that every action that a person performs in his body is a thought being planted in the mind. *Meenasana* will plant confident and joyful thoughts into the deep recesses of your mind.

Bring your arms above your head and stretch out through your spine. Point and flex your feet. Before coming up to touch your toes, squeeze your pelvic floor muscles, contract your navel center, and bring your chin to the chest to support your lower back. Come up to touch your toes with an exhalation. Sit up.

Come to standing. Bring your heels together, but separate your feet apart. You should experience relaxation in your legs. Press down through both the heel and the ball of your feet. Your shoulders are open, shoulder blades down and hands at the heart in *vanekom mudra*. Allow that new flow of blood, lymph and prana to circulate through your legs.

The 5th Asana – *Nindra Kokkuasana*, or *Uttanasana*, Standing Crane

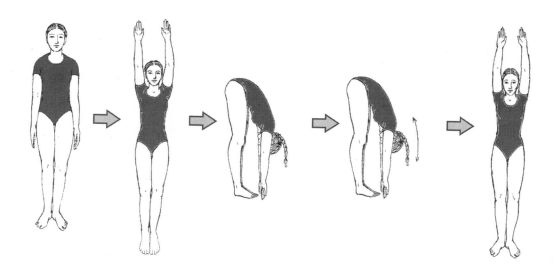

It is important to remember that when we are in an upright position, the bones of the axial skeleton should be in a balanced position. The appropriate body alignment is one in which the head, vertebrae, pelvic girdle and legs are in a balanced position. The feet should be brought parallel for this standing forward bend. With the heels together and feet apart, the thighs are rotated laterally and will resist deep bending and can accentuate imbalances throughout the foundation of the body. Do not lock your knees. Press down through the heel and the ball of both feet and feel the little toe touch the floor. Exerting pressure evenly through the foot will keep you from hyper-extending your knees.

Be Cautious: The movement of forward bending should come from the hip socket. Bending forward at the waist creates a downward pull of gravity, which pulls the vertebrae apart. There is less support in the lumbar region. Standing and touching toward your toes compresses the invertebrate disks of the lower back, and bouncing can aggravate low back problems and can even play a role in the development of disk problems. Gravity accelerates the movement forward.

It is especially important to protect the integrity of the disks and lower back in this posture by balancing strength with flexibility and avoiding strain. We can support the pose by keeping the abdominal muscles tightened, the pelvic floor lifted and the breath smooth and deep. Thus, we are utilizing the back muscles, abdominal muscles, the respiratory and pelvic diaphragms, and the *prana* to protect the spinal vertebrae.

Many people have tight hamstrings and hips, and tight connective tissue from the bottom of their feet, up the back side of the legs and along the spine to the base of the skull. This standing forward bend stretches the spinal cord, increasing pliability and flexibility of the spinal vertebra and rejuvenating the nerves. The whole of the back of the body, the bones, muscles and ligaments, tendons of the legs, torso and neck are stretched, increasing circulation. The sciatic nerve is stretched. Contraction of the abdomen and the gentle kriyas stimulate circulation and reduces fatty deposits in the belly. The pose strengthens the reproductive glands and the function of the liver, spleen and kidneys. It can be beneficial for those suffering from depression or a quick temper, as the pose soothes brain cells and can bring peace if held for about five minutes. There is an increase of blood flow into the brain and improved circulation into the thyroid and parathyroid glands. The heart rate slows. Vitality increases both to the body and mind.

****

Bring your feet parallel and hip distance apart. Spread your toes to better balance your weight. Your legs are straight. Tighten your thighs; both your hamstrings and quadriceps are contracted. Press down through the heel and the ball of the feet, the little toe touching the floor. Squeeze the pelvic floor muscles, tightening those muscles you would tighten to stop urination (*mulabandha*) and contract your abdominal muscles, tightening the lower abdominals. With these muscles engaged in contraction, you will feel an immediate strengthening in the lower back, a lengthening in the spine and an increase of strength. Keep these muscles tightened as you breathe in and out. Do not hold the abdominal muscles so tightly that it causes you to hold your breath.

Inhale deeply. Extend your arms above your head, shoulder blades down. Extend fully through the arms and fingertips. Press down through the heels and the balls of your feet, tightening your inner thigh muscles. This movement pushes against the effects of gravity. You may experience your muscular energy rising.

Bend forward at the hip socket, extending out with the arms and lengthening through the spine, pushing out with the buttocks. Stop the movement when the back is horizontal to the floor. Gravity will accelerate the movement, so keep pressing through the floor and extending through your arms. Keep the pelvic floor muscles and navel center engaged.

Imagine that you are directing the energy of the breath through the spine, from the coccyx through the cervical vertebrae for several breaths. Your head, neck and spine is in a straight line. Take deep breaths. When you experience the support of the breath, continue to bend forward. Relax your head and neck completely, interlace your fingers, invert your palms, and gently move up and down in a small pulsing movement with the palms reaching toward the floor. Many people have tight hamstrings, hips and connective tissue, which limits this movement. You can encourage muscular release with the gentle micro-movements, but don't bounce. Never force the stretch. If you feel some tension or strain in your lower back bend your knees.

Relax deeper with each micro-movement. Your palms may or may not reach the floor. This is the "the *kriya* phase," a gentle repetition or pulsation without force or strain. These internal micro-movements massage the internal organs, reduce fatty tissue from the abdomen and release the stretch reflex, so that you will be able to deepen in the stretch.

Asana always require a balance of strength and flexibility. To keep that balance, continue to squeeze the pelvic diaphragm and contract the abdominal muscles and keep the breath smooth and deep, both in and out. Use the *ujjayi* breathing. These all add strength and support to the muscles of the back and encourage relaxation of tight muscles.

Stop the movement. Bend your knees deeply in order to bring your torso against your thighs and take hold of your ankles or the back of your legs. Breathe into the stretch. Massage the back of your knees to help release the stretch reflex. Massage the hamstrings and calf muscles. Press into the heels, lift your hips gently, and slowly begin to straighten your legs as far as you can comfortably. Keep your chest against the thighs as you begin to straighten the legs. If your chest lifts off your thighs, bend your knees again.

Explore the stretch with the breath. Relax your mind. Focus concentration on *svadhistana chakra* at the sacrum. Be aware of where the sensation of tension lies in the body. Mentally direct the inhalation right to the center of any tension and visualize it releasing with the exhalation. Consciously bring pure strength and vitality in with each inhalation and release tension with each exhalation. Lengthening the inhalation will increase strength. Lengthening the exhalation will release tension. Maintain the *ujjayi* breathing, as it will help you to remain aware of the sensations and allow you to deepen the pose. The sensations in a stretch can change in a moment. The outside of your body is tensed and taut, yet internally you may experience fluidity, a sense of movement, as *prana* flows freely through the energy channels. Back out of any stretch if you experience pain or an increase in discomfort. Bend your knees more or come slowly out of the pose altogether. You can choose to stay with an intense stretch if it feels "good" to you.

Ask yourself if you can relax more in the pose. Relax the leveraging with you arms. Relax your head, neck, face. Breathe and visualize sending that downward flowing energy (*apana*) from the root chakra through the legs and feet. Relax your mind as well as emotions by mentally saying "let go" when you notice or feel their resistance expressed, for example with thoughts like, "I can't do this" or "I'm tired of this" or other feelings of agitation.

Slowly release the arms and hang for a moment, breathing. If your lower back muscles are weak, soften your legs and bring your hands to your waist. Bring your shoulders back and down and with the strength of your shoulders bring yourself back up. Continue to consciously support your back muscles with your pelvic diaphragm, abdominal muscles and breathe. If your back is strong, soften the knees and, pressing your feet into the floor, extend your arms and come up to standing in one inhalation. Reach upward, stretching through your arms and fingers and pressing down through your feet, holding the stretch for three more breaths.

Bend your elbows, and bring your hands into *vanekom mudra* at the heart. Heels come together with your feet separated. Relax standing for thirty seconds. Open to the qualities of this asana. *Nindra* (standing) *Kokkuasana* (crane) soothes the brain cells and brings vitality to the body and mind and a calm, peaceful state. The pose is good for relief of physical or mental fatigue, mental depression, insomnia, or lack of concentration.

The 6th Asana – Vilasana, or Dhanurasana, The Bow (counterpose)

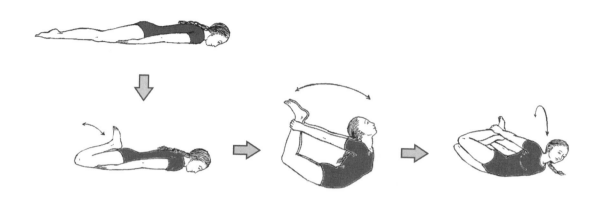

Vilasana, or **Bow Pose**, is a deep back-bending posture, which reconditions the whole of the alimentary canal. The abdominal organs and muscles and liver, gallbladder, and spleen, kidneys, small intestines and colon are all massaged. The Bow Pose supports circulation, respiration, digestion and elimination and reproduction. The pancreas and adrenal glands are stimulated and toned, which helps to balance their secretions. It has been used therapeutically for years to manage diabetes, as it facilitates circulation in the pancreas, which can help stabilize blood sugar levels. It has been found useful for people with asthma, as it frees energy in the sympathetic nerves in the chest and neck, which generally improves respiration. The parasympathetic nervous system is stimulated and all the glands benefit from the stretch of the bow. The spine is conditioned and realigned, and the ligaments, muscles and nerves are stretched and stimulated. It strengthens both the upper and lower extremities. It is helpful in reducing excess weight around the abdomen. The Bow Pose is one of the most powerful postures for releasing tension and increasing overall energy in the body. This posture can strongly stimulate solar plexus energy.

****

Release down onto the front of your body, placing your arms alongside (palms upward) and bring your chin to the floor. Your feet are hip distance apart.

The first stage: On your belly, with your arms along side of your body, your chin on the floor, repeatedly "kick" your buttocks with your heels. Kick both heels to the buttocks on the exhalation. Return the legs to the floor on inhalation. Continue for at least thirty kicks. You can choose to kick one leg to the buttocks at a time. This movement reduces tension in the thighs and gives flexibility to the waist and tones the sacro-illiac area of the spine. It can help to reduce inertia in the body and overcome laziness. It also strengthens the knee joints, increases the circulation of senovial fluid inside them, and consequently helps prevent and heal them from injuries and arthritis.

Second stage: Reach back and take hold of both of your ankles or your feet. Press your feet backward in your hands. Feel the traction in your arms and shoulders as the chest and head are lifted as high as possible. Your thighs may remain on the floor, allowing the back muscles to remain passive. Breathe. Squeeze the pelvic floor muscles and pull your navel toward the spine, then inhale and lift both your chest and thighs upward. Your shoulders should not be up toward your ears. The shoulder blades should not be slammed together. Keep the back open to allow energy to flow freely. Exhale and return your chest and thighs to the floor. Allow yourself to come in and out of the pose a few times so that your backbend deepens comfortably. Then, lift up into the full bow. Lift your chest, head and thighs upward, holding the pose, while breathing smoothly. Keep your legs and knees parallel and your back open. Do not over-extend your neck. The abdomen supports your entire body on the floor. Keep the pelvic floor muscles (*mulabandha*) contracted and your navel center tightened.

Third stage: Begin rocking backward and forward. Inhale as you rock backward and exhale as you rock forward. Bring through the spine to add more strength. Continue at least nine times. Return to center, and then rock to the right side. Hold the position, breathing and stretching and extending the bow. Breathe deeply, energizing your spine. Roll back to center and then over to the left side and hold the position stretching and extending the bow. Breathe. Keep the pelvic floor lifted and navel center tight. Roll now a few times back and forth from the right and to the left. Come back to center. Release down, still holding your feet or ankles. Relax.

Fourth stage: Tighten your pelvic floor and navel center. Inhale deeply and lift up once again into the full Bow. Allow the *prana* to support you in the lift and in the holding. Inhale bringing energy up the spine as you inhale. Feel the expansion of energy in the chest as you exhale. This is a tonic for the whole body.

Release the pose and relax onto the floor. Your body is still lying prone. Place your arms along side of your body. Turn your head so your right cheek is on the floor. Notice your breath. If it has speeded up, slow it down. Actively let go any discomfort, tension or sense of effort or frustration with your exhalations for at least thirty seconds. Release your head so the left cheek is on the floor and continue to relax for another thirty seconds. Stay focused on the inner sensations. The Bow Pose is one of the most powerful postures for releasing tension and increasing overall energy in the body. Relax well for several minutes, so that the toxins will have adequate time to be moved into the organs of elimination.

To come out of the relaxation, bring your chin back to the floor, with your hands along side of the shoulders, your toes pressed into the floor, and push up onto your hands and knees. Shift your weight backward and sit back on your feet. Fully extend your arms out in front of you. Place your hands flat on the floor. Open your armpits. Focus and breathe into your back.

Press down into your fingers and palms and press the toes into the floor. Lift your buttocks upward, creating a triangle with the floor. Shift your weight backward. Come up on your toes and stretch through the back of your body. Then, press the outside edge of your feet toward the floor (i.e., Mountain Pose, Downward-facing Dog, in Sun Salutation). Breathe and feel the whole backside of the body stretch.

Bring your right leg through the arms to the right hand and the left leg to the left hand. Bring your hands to the chest in *vanekom mudra* and slowly roll up to standing. Relax deeply in the streaming energy, while standing still, aligning, grounding and centering.

The 7th Asana – *Vibareetakarani*, Topsy-Turvey Pose, or "Opposite Doing" Pose

The heart and lung region is the center focus of *Vibareetankaraniasana*. Awareness, the breath and the center of gravity is concentrated at the heart. Is it said that *Vibareetankarani* is practiced to open the heart to love and compassion. The posture increases circulation to all the glands of the body. The cerebrum is invigorated. The cells in the muscles, skin, and face are nourished. Digestion and elimination function more efficiently and the reproductive glands are strengthened. Strain and fatigue in the head, legs and feet is relieved. This pose develops vitality and stamina.

****

Come onto your back with your head, neck and spine in a straight line. Bend your knees, folding your thighs over the abdomen and loosen the joint of your feet; stretch and wiggle the toes; flex the feet; rotate your ankles in both directions. Take time with this stage to open the joints in the feet and to stretch connective tissues and remove stagnant lymph and stimulate the return of venous blood.

Bring your arms to the floor along side your body. Breathe into the spine. Tighten your pelvic floor muscles and your abdominal muscles. Extend your legs upward toward the ceiling. Press your hands down onto the floor and lift your buttocks and back off the floor, vertebra by vertebra. Angle your legs towards your head. Do not lift the thoracic vertebrae (behind the heart) too high off the ground.

Bring your hands against the sacrum (the flat, triangular portion of the lower spine, of five-fused vertebrae, just above the coccyx). You can alternatively bring your hands to the outside of the hips, cupping them. Bring your elbows close to each other. Tip your pelvis forward so that your shoulders and arms share the weight of the body with the hands. The weight of the body should rest evenly between the hands, elbows and the shoulders, and the back is suspended between the shoulders and the hips. The center of gravity is in the chest, in the space of the heart. Breathing is very comfortable. The chin does not press against the chest and the head is free to move.

If you prefer, you can bring your legs more to the vertical position from the hips. Relax the feet. If you feel too much pressure in the elbows then angle the legs more towards the head, or you can try breathing into the tension at the elbows to release it. Be aware that the more you push the legs to a vertical position, the more the weight will shift to the neck. The legs should be positioned so there is no strain in the elbows or in the neck. This should be a relaxed posture.

The legs are straight, but in a passive stretch. The circulation drains blood from the feet and the legs moving it into the chest. The heart and lungs benefit from receiving more than the usual amount of blood.

This inversion is deeply relaxing and deeply purifying. Connect with that relaxing quality. Close your eyes and be still.

Bring your tongue up against the soft palate and focus your attention there for a few moments. Begin to silently chant the bija mantra *yum*, for opening the spiritual heart. Let the mantra draw your attention to the space of the heart. Begin to breathe the mantra in a circular pattern into and out through the heart center in the spine.

With each inhalation mentally vibrate *yumm*. Feel the energy release from the roof of the mouth and travel down to the heart center in the spine. With each exhalation mentally vibrate *yumm* upward through what you experience as the heart in the front of the body and back to the throat. Keep your awareness on the changing sensations, which accompany breathing this mantra through the heart.

Yummy! You may experience spontaneous contractions or pulsations. This spiritual center relates to altruistic love, to expansion and to the indefatigable nature of spirit. The heart center must be open if you are to experience your infinite self. Feel the vibration of the mantra sweetening the heart and drawing in a sublime energy.

To come out of the posture, place your arms on the floor close to the body, press down into your hands and slowly lower your spine down, vertebra by vertebra. When the buttocks reach the floor, extend your legs upward. Hold them there for a minute, aware of the downward flow of energy into your navel center. Maintain straight legs and the contraction of the pelvic and abdominal muscles. Release your legs slowly to the floor with abdomen and pelvic floor muscles tightened. If you experience any lower back strain, bend your knees and take you feet to the floor. Relax completely on your back in shavasana.

Breathe deeply and let go any sense of discomfort - physical or emotional - which might arise. Notice the quality of your breath. Remain aware of inner sensations.

Reach your arms above your head and stretch out in both directions, flexing your feet. Inhale and stretch again. Exhale, tightening your pelvic and abdominal muscles, bring your chin into your chest, come up to touch your toes, and then sit up.

> ### The 8th Asana - *Pathi Meenasana,* or *Ardha Matsyasana,* Half Fish Pose
> ### (counterpose)

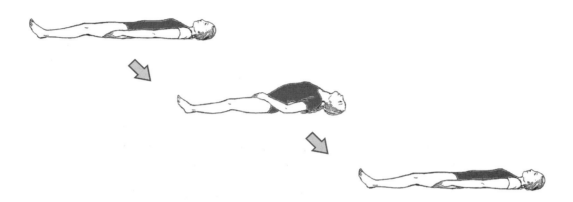

Vibareethankarani (Topsy Turvey) and *Pathi Meenasana* (Half Fish) are both good postures to do at night before bedtime, to help ease you into a deep and restful slumber. The Half Fish helps to encourage deep breathing and restful sleep. It will benefit someone who suffers from asthma as it relaxes the muscles that can tighten around the bronchioles and restrict the air passageway. The glands in the body are strengthened and metabolism is balanced. The pose balances the sympathetic nervous system and parasympathetic nervous system and lowers blood pressure. It is a pose that can be done in your bed for a minute or two just before sleep.

The pose can be used effectively to initiate changes in the psyche, if regularly held for ten minutes or longer, in combination with positive autosuggestion. Half Fish can be held comfortably by placing a firm pillow, bolster or rolled blanket under the upper back. A towel can be rolled and placed under the neck or pinned around the neck for support. The arms are stretched out from the shoulders. The chest and neck should remain lifted and opened and the shoulders relaxed. One should be able to rest in the pose in deep physical and mental comfort. When held for longer periods, the Half Fish Pose stimulates endorphins and helps to control depression.

****

Make sure you are sitting on your sitting bones (ischial tuberosity) with your legs extended fully to prepare for *Pathi Meenasana.* Bring your forearms down by your body and release back onto them. Aim the sitting bones (these are the bony projections at the lower end of the body) downward and pubic bone forward. Notice how this tilts the pelvis so that the sacrum moves upward toward the waist). Engage the pelvic floor muscles and tighten your navel center, bringing it toward the spine. Begin spinal breathing. Bring energy up the spine as you inhale and feel that energy expand as you exhale. Lift your chest from the heart, look upward, and carefully release back.

Lift your chin and release the back of the head towards the floor. Lower the crown of your head onto the floor if you are able to comfortably. Lifting the heart will arch the thoracic spine more than the lumbar spine. Allow your feet and thighs to drop open, to rotate laterally. Keep your chest and neck lifted with your shoulders relaxed.

You can continue to support yourself with your forearms, or place your arms on your thighs, or bring them into prayer pose (*vanekom mudra*) at your heart center. Breathe. Alternately, you might invert your hands in prayer pose, so that your fingertips touch your sternum and gently tap on your chest at the thymus gland to stimulate the immune system. The Fish Pose strengthens all the glands in the body and balances metabolism.

Hold the pose in stillness. Focus on the space of the heart. Notice how the full breathing is moving energy in the spine towards the neck and head. You should be able to rest deeply in comfort in this version of the Fish Pose. If you experience discomfort, slowly come out of the pose. Holding Fish Pose for extended lengths of time can have deeply spiritual effects as the heart and upper *adharas* (centers of psychic energy) are stimulated to give and receive universal energy and love. (Don't swallow or cough or sneeze while in this pose as you may gag. Also, do not do the pose if you have fever or a headache).

To come out of the pose bring your forearms back to the floor. Press down into your elbows and forearms, slide your chin toward the chest and bring your head and neck back to the floor with great care and control. Relax on your back and turn your head from side to side to release any blocked energy at the throat. Stay aware of internal sensations. When the posture is released, *prana* is encouraged to reverse its normal flow and descend. This brings about pranic stillness and mental silence. Notice the quality of the breath. You should notice that your breath has become lighter, more subtle.

Consciously release any discomfort, which might arise with an exhalation.

Stretch your arms above your head, point and flex your toes and stretch out through the spine. Tighten your pelvic floor, and abdominal muscles, bring your chin into your chest and exhaling come up to touch your toes. Sit up. Cross your legs and come up to standing. Bring your heels together, feet apart. Spread your toes. Press through your feet. Open your shoulders and bring your hands into *vanekom mudra* at the heart.

The 9th Asana - *Kalapoyasana* or *Halasana*, **The Plough Pose**

The health of the body is determined by the flexibility of the spine. One determinant of physical aging is spinal flexibility or rigidity. The next posture, *Kalapoyasana*, or Plough Pose, is an exceptional posture for general health and well-being. It is the perfect counter-balance to the normal positioning of the spine. It stretches the spinal cord, flushing the spinal nerves with blood. It can relieve upper and lower back pain caused by strain. The pose releases tight shoulder and neck muscles.

The Plough Pose increases circulation of the blood throughout the body. It improves blood supply to the heart. It is good for the health of the thyroid and parathyroid gland, and the thymus gland, promoting physical vitality and emotional stability. It is helpful in correcting poor metabolism. Blood flow to the brain is improved, benefiting both the pituitary and pineal glands. The neck lock will slow blood pressure, induce relaxation and help to eliminate mental laziness. It can increase one's capacity for work.

A word of caution: the Plough Pose places a great amount of pressure on the delicate bones in the cervical vertebrae. As we age, these vertebrae degenerate. It is of extreme importance to **go** very slowly into the pose, not to jeopardize the integrity of the vertebral column. Once in the pose, keep your head and neck absolutely still. Plough Pose is contra-indicated for those who have weakness in the cervical vertebrae or arthritis of the neck.

****

Lie flat on your back, and align head, neck and spine. Fold your knees over your abdomen and loosen the joints in the feet. Spread and flex the toes five times. Point and flex your feet five times, and then rotate your ankles in both directions, five times.

Contract your pelvic floor and your abdominal muscles and raise your legs straight up. Breathe into the spine. Inhale and draw the breath up the spine. Exhale and let the breath expand in the body. Extend your legs at an angle over your head. Notice the stretch in the hamstring muscles. Lengthen the neck. Press into your hands and lift your buttocks. Keep your attention on the stretch in the hamstrings as you slowly lower your legs over your head.

Bring your hands to your lower back. Your elbows should be placed on the floor, as close to each other as you can bring them, in order to lift the back of the neck off the floor. Creating a triangle between the shoulders and the back of the head will help prevent you from straining the muscles in the neck or putting too much pressure on the cervical vertebrae. Bending at the hips in this way helps to relieve stomach gas, and gives the abdominal organs a good massage.

Continue to breathe through your spine as you direct your feet towards the floor, behind the head. Don't force your feet to the floor. Sense the blood flooding into the back of your legs as your continue the stretch. Be aware of the alignment of your head, neck and spine. If you cannot easily bring your feet to the floor, let them rest at a comfortable height from the floor. Alternately, you can release your knees onto your forehead center.

Use the kriyas, the micro-movements, and gently pulse in the direction of your feet. Allow the micro-movements to release your back muscles and bring tone and suppleness to your spine. You can use these movement even if your knees are on your forehead center, as if to massage the forehead center. Use the *ujjayi* breath with the spinal breathing.

Stopping the kriyas, relax into the pose. You may wish to keep your hands on your back for support or prefer to bring your arms to the floor, interlacing your hands and drawing the shoulder blades closer to strengthen the triangular base of support for your neck.

Let your attention be drawn into the sound of the breath, as it moves through your throat. Remain concentrated to stimulate the subtle center in the throat. Close your eyes, breathe and relax deeply in any sensation you are experiencing. As you breathe, the movement of the diaphragm is massaging the internal organs. You may experience a tingling sensation over the body and had a sense of various energy fields.

Next, bend your knees and bring them on either side of your head. If you can do this comfortably, hold the position for several breaths. This variation with the ears pressed against by the knees will encourage deep relaxation in the torso, arms and legs.

To begin to come out of the pose, while pressing the palms into the floor, slowly lower the back and buttocks down. Raise the legs again to the vertical position. Breathe in this position for several breaths and become aware of the energy flowing into the navel center. Engaging your abdominal and pelvic floor muscles, release your straight legs to the floor, as slowly as possible, to strengthen your navel center. (**Remember**: if your back feels weak, just bend your knees and bring your feet to the floor).

Feel the release of energy and its assimilation throughout the body. Relax on your back into *shavasana* and stay attuned to the qualities of your breath and to the inner sensations. Each posture should be taking you into a deeper sense of relaxation, into a quieted and relaxed body and mind.

Stretch your arms out above your head and stretch fully. Point and flex your feet and come up to touch toward the toes. Come to a sitting position.

The 10th Asana – *Paambuasana*, or *Bhujangasana*, the Serpent (counterpose)

The *Paambuasana*, or Serpent (Cobra) Pose, builds a sense of inner strength, both physical and mental. It, like the Plough Pose before it, will relieve tension in the shoulders, neck and upper back (thoracic spine), and elongate and tone the spine. The Plough and Serpent Poses harmonize the body by strengthening the spine and by moving energy from the root center (*muladhara*) at the base of the spine into the higher energy center (*ajna*) between the brows. They work to connect the upper and lower body energies and balance the positive and negative energies. The Serpent Pose refines this electro-magnetic power in the body. Serpent Pose stimulates the cranial nerves, relieving stress and gives a boost of energy, both mental and physical.

Serpent Pose helps maintain normal healthy spinal alignment. Regular practice can even adjust a displacement in the spinal column. Serpent Pose can correct a rounded spine and relieve an aching back. The whole spine receives a steady pull anteriorly. The deep muscles of the back are alternately contracted and relaxed in working the pose in both ways so these muscles are exercised and nourished with blood, which aids in health and elasticity of the spine.

Serpent Pose warms the whole system and improves neuromuscular coordination. Arching the spine improves circulation in the back and increases communication between the nerves, the brain and body. The thirty-two pairs of spinal nerves and the two gangliated cords of sympathetic nerves are all stimulated. Stretching the neck back in this position can help to normalize thyroid and parathyroid functioning. It is used therapeutically to help prevent migraines.

Serpent Pose opens and expands the chest and shoulders, benefiting the lung and heart function. The stretch makes the blood flow faster, allowing the organs to receive an extra supply of oxygenated blood. It has been shown to lower cholesterol in clinical studies and so is helpful in cardiovascular disease. The thymus gland is also stimulated in this pose, helping to strengthen immune function. It stretches the abdominal muscles and increases intra-abdominal pressure. The stretch and pressure in the abdominal region helps to relieve constipation, and strengthens the reproductive system, toning the ovaries and uterus, and promotes the healing of menstrual and other gynecological disorders. In addition, Serpent Pose massages the liver and kidneys, gallbladder, spleen, adrenal glands and pancreas, which is beneficial for efficient functioning.

****

Position yourself prone on your mat. Bring your arms along side your body with your palms upward, your chin on the floor and your head in line with the spine. Tighten the pelvic floor muscles (*mulabandha*) and draw your navel center toward the spine, tightening your lower abdominal muscles to support your lower back. Keep these contractions throughout the performance of the asana. Your legs can be together, but widen the space between them as much as you need to in order to take pressure off of your lower back. Contract the inner thigh muscles (adductors).

With these contractions your pelvis will feel stable as you lift your torso off the floor with your inhalation. If you feel pressure in your sacrum and lumbar spine, widen your legs a bit more. Your arms should remain relaxed along side your body. Lengthen your spine as you lift your head and chest off the ground. Look forward. Utilize spinal breathing to internally support the pose. Each inhalation draws energy up the spine as you lift your upper body. On exhalation, lower your torso and chin back down to the floor, energy flowing throughout your body. Your breathing is continuous and coordinated with your movements. Each inhalation lifts your upper body and each exhalation bringing your upper body back to the floor.

You are using the muscles in your lower back, but also utilizing your abdominal muscles, adductor muscles, gluteus muscles, and pelvic and respiratory diaphragm. Your spine should feel strong as you move up and down on the breath. It is important to coordinate your movements with your breathing and to keep awareness in your spinal breathing. Be conscious of the upward flowing *prana* that strengthens the lift, and the outward expanding *prana* that supports the movement back to the floor. Continue this stage until the spine feels open and strong.

In the second stage, bring your hands to the level of your shoulders, with your thumbs at the base of the breast and your elbows held close into the body. Your shoulder blades move back and down. If you find your back is very tight, you can allow your hands to slide a bit forward or take them a bit further from your body. These hand positions will support the back and shift the work from the back to the shoulders.

Make certain that you are still squeezing the pelvic floor muscles, pulling the navel in toward the spine, tightening the inner thigh muscles. Press into the pubic triangle as you lift upward. Lengthen your spine as you lift upward with your inhalation, raising your vertebrae one by one, instead of giving a full backward curve to your spine all at once. Keep your pelvis on the floor. Your head and neck are aligned with the shoulders, eyes straight ahead. Your shoulder blades are back and down. Your elbows remain slightly bent so that your heart is pressing forward. This position creates a deeper arch in the thoracic vertebra, taking some pressure off the lumbar spine.

As you hold the pose, continue the spinal breathing. Energy is being directed up the spine with each inhalation. If you need to come in and out of the pose do so by coordinating the movement with the breath.

As a variation, twist in the Serpent to increase the stretch in the abdomen, muscles of the back and the intestines and increase your inhalation. Inhaling, slowly twist your head and the upper portion of your torso to the right. Try to twist far enough around to see your right foot. Exhale as you return to the center. Inhaling, twist around toward your left . Exhale as you return to the center. Try to keep your back relaxed and receive this nice diagonal stretch. Keep your navel near to the floor. Repeat a few more times.

Return to the center position and, again engaging the pelvic floor and navel center, rise into the full Serpent. Keep your elbows held in toward the body, your shoulders are open. Visualize sparkling, silvery white energy rising in the spine with each in-breath and expanding in the body with each out-breath. As the deep and superficial muscles of the back contract, the spine will bend deeper into the backbend. The spine is being flushed with blood and energy. As you feel the spine release, slowly extend the neck, lifting your chin. Roll your eyes up to the space between the brows. Direct that sparkly energy up the spine into this space. Energy rises with each inhalation and expanding at the Third Eye on exhalation. Visualize the spine as an open channel for this flow of energy. Feel that this breathing pattern is supporting you effortlessly.

With the spine still lengthened, slowly lower your body onto the floor. Move as slowly to the floor, as you went up into the backbend. Bring your legs together and your arms forward, on either side of your head. Bring your palms together. Your forehead touches the floor and your body forms one straight line. You are in the stage of Complete Surrender. This is a posture to surrender the contracted perspective of the ego to that of your soul. Focus your aspiration on the Lord, whose abode is above the head, with outstretched hands, palms together in prayer position. When life's problems become too burdensome, practice this posture and pray, "Not my will, but thy will be done."

Tighten your pelvic floor (*mulabandha*) and tighten the area of the navel center, and again visualize your spine, as an open channel for the awakening and rising energies in the body.

Inhale. Use ujjayi and spinal breathing. At the top of the inhalation, open your arms wide, lifting your head and chest off the floor. Your feet remain on the floor. Exhale bringing your arms, chest and head back to the original position. Clap the hands together as you release your torso and forehead back onto the floor in compete surrender. Clap your hands with intention to awaken the kundalini shakti. Repeat this movement five times. Your core temperature increases with each breath.

Bring your arms back to the side of your body. Turn your head to one side. Allow time for the new circulation of energy to be assimilated. Notice the quality of the breath. The breath should now be very subtle. Turn your head to the other side and continue to relax for an additional fifteen to thirty seconds.

Bring your hands to your shoulders, bring your toes into the floor and push up on the hands and knees. Shift your weight back, extending your arms. Open your armpits and stretch your lower back in an extended child pose. Press into your fingers and palms and lift your buttock up to create a triangle with the floor. Come up onto your toes. Again shift your weight backward. Bring the outside edge of your feet down toward the floor. Energy will flow freely through the back side of the body. Breathe.

Bring your right foot to your right hand and your left foot to the left hand. Bring your hands together into prayer pose (*vanekom mudra*) at the heart and roll up slowly to the standing position. Open the shoulders. Bring your heels together with the feet separated. Your legs relax. Notice the sensations in the body.

The 11th Asana - *Yoga Mudrasana*, Yogic Symbol Pose

Yoga Mudrasana builds a strong abdominal wall and is beneficial for many abdominal ailments as it give a powerful compression to the abdomen. It increases circulation to the pancreas and helps improve its functioning. Intra-abdominal pressure with the closed fists in *nabi mudra* pressed against the abdomen creates an internal muscular massage, which regenerates organs of the abdomen and intensifies peristalsis. Increased circulation to the pelvic region strengthens reproductive organs. *Nabi mudra* massages the liver, gall bladder, spleen, small and large intestines and kidneys improving function.

Yoga Mudrasana stretches the spine, gently toning the spinal nerves, the sacral and lumbar nerves in particular and contributes to overall good heath. The deep back muscles of the erector spinae, which support the lumbar spine and the superficial latissimus dorsi of the mid-back are strengthened. The kriyas stimulate the parasympathetic nerve fibers in the lower back and the sympathetic nerves of the mid-back. The movement forward releases pressure on the spinal nerves giving them a profound stretch and also stimulates all the nerves of the body to the brain, improving function. When the chest is expanded, the joints in the shoulders and the heart and lungs benefit.

Sitting in lotus pose (*padmasana*) strengthens the joints in the legs and redirects energy upward. It creates a balance in the body that encourages physical and mental stillness. Practice of Yogamudrasana increases pranic energy, conserves it and increases the power of concentration. The pose calms the adrenal system and induces a deep state of relaxation. It is good for mental stress and strain and general tiredness and fatigue. It is said that *Yoga Mudrasana* reduces fever in the body and passion in the mind. *Yoga Mudrasana* is "psychic union pose." It improves the positive and negative energies in the body, bringing a cooperative spirit to physical and mental energies and a general sense of tranquility to the body and mind. It is powerful enough to arouse energy at the base of the spine. It stimulates all the adharas from *muladhara* to *ajna*. It can develop an awareness of psychic energy. It is powerful preparation for meditation. It has the power to connect you to your subtle self.

****

Come to an easy crossed-leg seated position (*sukasana*) to prepare the hip joint for the full lotus. Make certain that you are sitting on the sitting bones (ischial tuberosity) and that your back is straight. Bring the soles of your feet together. On the exhalation, bring the heels as close to the body as comfortable. Begin to flutter your knees toward the floor. Feel the nice opening in your hips.

Take hold of your feet and bring your elbows against your thighs and lengthen your back, while releasing forward, exhaling. Do not use force. Try not to round your back. Visualize yourself breathing into your lower back and slowly releasing tension from your back and hip socket. Breathe. You can open your feet so the soles face upward and on exhalation, release a bit deeper. Imagine your chest releasing to the soles of your feet. You are increasing circulation in the pelvis. Keep extension in your spine. Inhale with the intention of increasing strength in the body. Exhale with the intention of relaxing tension in the muscles. Breathe and relax as much as you can for at least a minute. Slowly come up to sitting.

Bend your left knee, bringing both your arms around your leg to cradle it. Alternately, you can bring both wrists underneath your ankle. Gently rock the hip, to the left and to the right. Bring your leg as far as you can in both directions for at least thirty seconds. Then place the left foot as far over onto the right thigh as you can; your left ankle should be supported on the thigh. Rapidly rub or massage any tightness felt in the knee or hip. Hold the toes with the right hand, and lift the left knee upward and press it gently downward with the left hand. Coordinate the movement with your breathing, inhaling, lift your knee upward and exhaling press downward. Do not press your knee down to the floor if you feel tension in the knee cap; bring it only to a horizontal position. Relax your left leg and pat out any tension. Repeat these exercises on the other leg. Bend the right knee, taking right leg under the ankle or cradling it and rock it side to side. Place the right foot onto your left thigh and bring the right knee up and down, with the breath until the hip relaxes. Work with these stretches until you feel the musculature is warm and your hips are open enough to move safely into lotus pose or use a half lotus, sukasana (easy crossed-leg pose).

The Lotus: Sitting on your sitting bones, and with your spine straight, move into a full lotus. *Take hold of your right shin and ankle from underneath your leg, so you rotate the shin and thigh outward (don't grab your foot above your leg). Keeping your foot flexed, ease your right foot as high and as far over on top of your left thigh as you comfortably can so that your right ankle is supported on your thigh. If the ankle bends so that the sole of your foot faces up at you, the ankle is weakened and there is an excessive pull on the ligaments and cartilage of the knee. Bend your left knee, flex your left foot, take your left ankle and shin from underneath and slide your left leg on top of your right. Relax your feet. If you don't experience comfort and stability in this posture, release your left leg out and cross it under you. If you experience pain in the right leg, sit in sukasana, easy pose (both legs crossed under you).

Tighten your pelvic floor and the navel center. Take hold of the big toe of each foot, your chest and shoulders are open, your shoulder blades down, your elbows next to the body. Begin spinal breathing. Bend forward slowly. Allow the *ujjayi* breathing to release tension as you move your forehead toward the floor. Stop the forward moving if you feel tightening in the musculature and breathe. You can utilize the kriyas, micro-movements, little pulsations, to inch your way further into the stretch.

Relax into this forward bend. Your deep *ujjayi* spinal breathing will continue to lengthen the spine. The contraction in the pelvic floor and abdomen will support your lower back and begin to direct energy upward. Bring your forehead to the floor as you can comfortably. Continue to settle into the posture, just by working with the breath for one to two minutes. Come up slowly, keeping your spine elongated.

Begin the second stage with *nabi mudra*. Bring your thumbs inside your palms, fingers folding over. Bring the fists together, the knuckles fitting in such a way that they can roll like gears meshing together. This massages the nerve endings and acupressure points between the base of the fingers and relaxes the hands. The hands can be held horizontally or vertically. This can help to conserve nervous energy that is normally released through the hands.

Now, bring your fists on either side of the navel center. Press deeply. Bend forward, slowly, lengthening not rounding your lower back. Keep your buttocks on the floor. Use micro-movements, little pulsations, in order to release forward more deeply. Again, bring your forehead to the floor and breathe, using the *ujjayi* and spinal breathing. Inhale and exhale slowly. Exhale away any discomfort. Be patient and persistent. The nerves will become strong. The electromagnetic power of the body and the working capacity of the body will increase if you practice this regularly. Relax in the pose as long as you like. Sit up.

To begin the third stage, again, tighten your pelvic floor muscles (*mulabandha*) and your navel center. Cross your arms behind your back and reach around as far as you can at your waist. Take hold of the toes on one or both sides, if you are flexible enough. Drop your chin to your chest. This creates a fully-banded lotus. (Alternately, you can bring your arms behind you, interlace your fingers, locking them, taking your shoulder blades close).

Bend forward, breathing out as you move. Begin with small micro-movements, bringing your forehead closer and closer to the floor in front of you. The aim is to bring your forehead on the floor to stimulate the flow of energy mid-brain, into ajna. Breathe deeply and smoothly.

If your arms are interlaced behind you, bring them up as high as possible toward the head. Keep your fingers interlaced and shoulder blades close. A full stretch in the shoulders creates a muscular lock in the arms that helps move energy upward. Draw your eyes to concentrate at the "third eye" space between the brows. Continue to hold your head still as you breathe in the spine. Continue to stretch your arms upward as you breathe. Do not force this. If there are irregularities in the breathing, relax the stretch in the arms.

To release out of the pose, slowly rise to center. Release your hands and place them on your knees. Notice the quality of the breath and the deepening stillness in body and mind. Rest in stillness.

Release the crossed legs, and stretch them out. Massage out any tension in the knees and pat out both sides of the legs. Rock them from side to side to release tension in the hips. Lie onto your back and release your head from side to side to release any blocked energy. Relax on your back in *shavasana* for thirty seconds. Then, bring your arms above your head and your legs together and stretch. Point and flex your toes as you stretch in both directions. Inhale and come up to touch your toes, with your pelvic floor and navel tightened to support your lower back and your chin to your chest, to support your neck.

The 12th Asana - *Pathi Chakrasana*, Half-Wheel Pose (counterpose)

Pathi-chakrasana, the Half-wheel Pose, is a dynamic and energizing backbend, which expands and stimulates the whole of the spine. *Pathi Chakrasana* aligns the vertebra, strengthens the neck, and tones the cervical, thoracic, lumbar and sacral regions of the spine. It balances positive and negative energies in the body, stretches and strengthens the spinal cord and brings flexibility to the spine. It brings a sense of youthful energy, lightness and buoyancy to the body. Even the senses, seeing, voice, hearing, taste and smell are said to improve through regular practice of this asana. The navel, heart and lungs are kept healthy. All the glands of the body are nourished, which in turn increases hormonal secretion and general health. The skin and lymph system benefit. The body itself can awaken to a new and alternative way of adapting to stress as it changes old patterns of muscle behavior. The practice of *Pathi Chakrasana* can affect powerful changes.

****

Bridge Pose is wonderful preparation for this deep back bend. It can also be an adequate substitute for the pose if you have weakness in your neck or wrists. Lie on your back. Bring your knees up with your feet on the floor. Your feet should be brought about 6 to 8 inches from your buttocks. Your knees are hip distance apart. Your feet aim straight ahead. Do not let your feet splay out to the sides. Take hold of your ankles (thumb inside, fingers holding the outer ankle) or place your arms along side of your body. Tighten your pelvic floor muscles and pull in your navel center. Press down through your feet and inhaling roll your buttocks and sacrum up off the floor, taking your spine up, vertebra by vertebra. Lift your pubic bone up, creating an arch in your back. Your inhaled breath directs energy upward from the base of the spine. Lift your navel and bring your chest high. Push your chest toward your chin, without moving the position of the feet or shoulders. On exhalation, release down to the floor, in the same precise way, vertebra by vertebra, nine to twenty-six times. Energy expands throughout the body as you exhale. On the last lift you can choose to hold the lifted position. Continue to hold in this modified posture, if your cervical vertebra, or wrists, or shoulders are weak or your back is tight. Keep your navel center lifted. Move the position of your hands. Bring your arms under you and interlace your fingers, bringing the shoulder blades close. Keep the contraction in the pelvic floor and abdomen. Continue the spinal breathing. Hold for two to five minutes. When you come out of the posture, relax in *shavasana*.

If your back muscles are warmed and your neck and wrists are strong, you do not need to begin with bridge pose. From the supine position, place your feet on the floor six to eight inches from your buttocks. Your hands are placed on either side of your head, elbows up, your fingers aim toward your feet. Your legs and feet are parallel. Squeeze the muscles of your pelvic floor and pull your navel center toward your spine. Begin spinal breathing. Press into the hands and feet and inhale as you lift your torso high enough to lift your head a few inches off the floor. Gently place the top of the head onto the floor. You are in a five-point stance. The weight is equally distributed between the both hands, both feet, and your head. Your pelvis is lifted high and your chest is pushed toward the chin. Keep breathing in the spine with ujjayi breathing. Keep your navel center lifted.

Holding this posture strengthens the back and neck muscles and its practice increases circulation to the brain, giving many of the benefits of the headstand. Be aware of the qualities of the breath and the aliveness of the inner body. Hold as long as you are holding it with strength and your breath is soft and free of strain.

To come out of the pose, press again into the hands and feet and lift your head up a few inches off the floor, bring your chin into your chest, and bring the back of your head onto the floor. Make sure your head, neck and spine is aligned as it releases to the floor. Relax on your back in *shavasana*. Move your head from side to side to release any blocked energy. Notice the quality of your breath and the increased flow of energy throughout the whole of the body. The body becomes more buoyant with this pose as if it is less affected by gravity. You should experience a deep sense of relaxation.

To stretch the spine, bring your legs together and your arms above your head. Point and flex your feet and stretch in both directions. Exhaling, chin in to chest, abdominals and pelvic floor tightened, come up to touch your toes and then sit up. Cross your right leg over your left and come to standing without the use of your hands. This strengthens the quadriceps, stimulates the liver and balances energy at the navel center. If this causes stress in the knee, use your hands. Bring your hands in *vanekom mudra* at the heart.

The 13th Asana - *Amarntha Kokkuasana,* **or** *Paschimottanasana,* **Sitting Crane Pose**

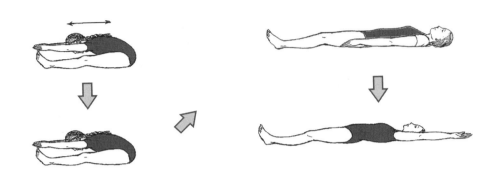

Amarntha Kokkuasana, Sitting Crane stimulates the spinal nerves and stretches all the posterior muscles of the body. This posterior stretch on the spine ensures that the nerve fibers and cell bundles of the sympathetic and parasympathetic spine passing through the disks are relaxed and energized. The elasticity of the spine is improved. The spine and spinal cord are stretched in a position parallel to the ground, relaxing the effects of the downward pull of gravity. Because the heart is kept under the spine and spinal cord, blood flow is increased into the heart, and so the heart is relaxed and refreshed. Blood circulation is increased throughout the body. This pose has been used clinically to help to reduce plaque in the coronary arteries and lower cholesterol. It can ease tension in the low back caused by a sway back or lordosis, if done passively with attention to alignment.

The pull on the great toes secures a full relaxation and a complete stretching of the posterior muscles of the legs. The hamstrings are stretched fully and it gives the sciatic nerve a good stretch. This stretch can slim buttocks and thighs. All the glands and muscles of the arms and legs are strengthened due to increased circulation. Sitting Crane Pose tones and massages the entire abdominal and pelvic region including the liver, pancreas and spleen, kidneys and adrenal glands, as well as the reproductive organs. Its regular practice is considered to be a panacea for a whole host of functional disorders involving digestion, elimination and reproduction.

This forward bend stretches the whole backside of the body and promotes connectedness between the upper and lower halves by balancing the flow of energy between them. It has considerable spiritual significance. It stimulates the flow of an abundance of dynamic energy. To master the pose one must be able to remain effortlessly in the asana for extended lengths of time. Listen for the *pranava,* (the sound of prana), Aum. It awakens kundalini shakti.

****

Sit on the floor with your legs extended in front of you. If your back is very tight, try sitting on a wedge or small cushion to lift your hips a bit. Bring your sitting bones onto the floor. You should be on your sitting bones, and your legs should be straight with your feet together and flexed. Tighten your thighs, contracting both quadriceps and the hamstring muscles. Tighten your abdominal muscles. *Do not contract the pelvic floor muscles; do not engage *mulabandha* in this pose. We want to encourage energy to flow downward through the legs.

Stretch your arms above your head and bring your shoulder blades downward. Inhale as you stretch up and exhale as you bend forward from the hip joint. Bring your lower back in front of the pelvis. The spine will arch gently, not become round. Focus is on lengthening in the lumbar spine, not rounding it. Your eyes should be kept open and your chin lifted. This will help you maintain a straight back. Continue spinal breathing with *ujjayi pranayama* to internally support and gently stretch your lower back.. Don't force the stretch.

When your arms are parallel to the floor, your hands reaching toward or above your feet, begin the "kriya phase," a gentle pulsing with the breath. Use a forward motion (not up and down). This phase creates internal micro-movements, which activate change at deep levels in the musculature of the spine. Do not force this stretch. The repeated movements of the kriyas aid removal of fatty tissue from the abdomen and massage the internal organs, increasing circulation in them. The kriyas can even stimulate change at emotional levels. For instance, if you place concentration at *manipura*, and coordinate the movement with the breath, you can visualize releasing tension and negativity from the belly with each exhalation

In the next stage, the movement phase ceases so that you can release in the pose. If you can, take hold of your big toe or the back of the flexed feet and lower your chest, so that your forehead touches your knees. The pull on the great toes or flexed feet secures a full relaxation and a full stretch of the posterior muscles of the legs. Close your eyes and focus your concentration at the energy center at the sacrum, to awaken *svadhisthana*. Breathe. *Prana* travels with awareness on the flow of the breath. If the epicenter of your mind is at one point, *prana* will be stimulated at that point. Do this only if you are steady and comfortable and experience a sense of stillness.

If you cannot easily reach your feet, take hold of your legs and continue to lengthen through your lower back. Do not let your back round. Keep the contraction in your thighs and your feet flexed to keep a stretch in the posterior muscles of the legs. Breathe in and out of the navel center with deep *ujjayi* breaths. Your belly expands with the inspiration and contracts with the expiration. Close your eyes and focus concentration on your sacrum. Be relaxed, there is no need to force this stretch.

Find a position in which you can remain in comfort for at least two minutes. Allow the releases to happen from the inside. When the back of your body is stretched firm and taut the vertebra column is stretched fully; you create space and increase the flow of *prana*. The *prana* begins to flow more freely to nourish and tone the spinal nerves and releases the stretch reflex, so both the musculature and the mind can relax. Let the stretch become less active, more passive and quite pleasurable.

Practice with Awareness. Notice the quality of your breath. Is your breath smooth and even? If your breath is irregular or feels restricted, then ease back up out of that stretch slightly. Find a position where the stretch feels good. The idea is to settle into the "sitting crane." It is an introverted pose. Stay present to the sensations in the body. If you are experiencing tension, the *prana* is blocked, so consciously nourish that area through the breath. While inhaling, imagine directing silvery energy right into tightness. While exhaling, let that silvery energy expand in the area and let go of all resistance or agitation.

Sitting Crane is a good antidote for mental and physical fatigue and lethargy. It is a posture of letting go and breaking free. Let go of obstacles that are making you tired. As you break through your physical resistances in this pose and find you can hold it for a longer time in comfort, you will find that you also break through resistance in your life. Hold the pose a little longer than you "want" to, and you can release the need to control everything in your life.

As you release out of the pose, open your eyes, lift your chin and accelerate the stretch. Your abdominal muscles should still be tight and your thighs contracted and your feet flexed. Reach out toward the space in front of you, as your bring your arms up above your head. Take a few deep breaths. Do you feel lines of energy flowing down your legs and up through your arms?

Drop your chin to your chest, and cross your arms over your chest to minimize pressure in the lower back, as you slowly roll your back to the floor. Relax on your back in shavasana. You may notice an increased flow of energy in the abdominal area, the hips, groins and thighs, or a deepening sense of relaxation. Stay focused on internal sensations. Release your head from side to side and relax well.

To stretch the spine, bring your legs together and your arms above your head. Point and flex your feet and stretch in both directions. Exhaling, with your chin in to your chest, abdominals and pelvic floor tightened, come up to touch your toes. Sit up.

14th Asana - *Vittelasana*, or *Shalabhasana*, Grasshopper Pose (counterpose)

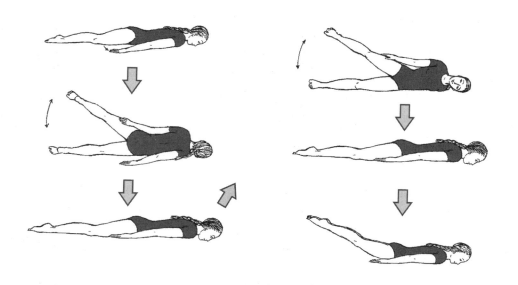

The *Vittelasana*, or Full Grasshopper Pose, works to stretch the abdomen and thighs and flushes the kidneys and releases pelvic tension. In addition, it is an ideal posture for opening the mid and upper back and hip areas. This asana relaxes tensions in the lower back caused by prolonged sitting, which can cause stress in the invertebrate disks. The stretching in this pose promotes spinal alignment and increases circulation to the disks, which is necessary for maintenance and repair. The lumbar and sacral nerves and the lower vertebrae are toned. The small of the back develops strength. Resting the chin on the floor during the posture extends the front of the neck and throat, stimulating circulation to the thyroid gland and helps regulate metabolism. The pressure on the heart increases blood output to all parts of the body, nourishing all the cells. During inhalation the diaphragm drops low against the viscera and so the intra-abdominal pressure is great. Digestion benefits and the liver, gallbladder, stomach, spleen, kidneys, small intestines, colon, urinary bladder, and prostrate gland are all strengthened. The posture invigorates the reproductive organs and benefits both semen and ovum. Menstrual problems are often relieved. The very sensitive small blood vessels receive an increase of better oxygenated blood. The navel is strengthened. Electromagnetic power of the body improves and vital energy is increased. The gluteus maximus are tightened and toned.

The first stage of the pose works primarily with energy in the *muladhara* and *svadhisthana* adharas, which may bring up issues surrounding our core need for safety, survival and sexuality. The Full Grasshopper works with *manipura* (solar plexus) energy, which may help increase the ability to sustain power. It, along with Sitting Crane, will work on "letting go" in areas where you might be holding back in life. The Full Grasshopper can express self-reliance and strength. It powerfully stimulates the energy center at the throat, *vishuddhi*, when the chin is stretched on the floor during the pose.

****

Lie on the right side of your body. Your body is in a straight line. Shift your right arm behind you, rolling your right shoulder out of the way so you are lying on the right side of your chest, not on your right shoulder. Place your left arm on the left hip or in front of your body. You can bend your bottom leg (right) to create a broader base of support. Your head should be straight over the shoulder and resting on the floor. Tighten your pelvic floor muscles and pull your navel toward the spine.

Flex both feet. Lift and lower your left leg in sync with your breath. Inhale lifting and exhale lowering your leg. Lead with your left heel. Do not lean forward. With your feet flexed you will be not be able to raise your leg as high as you could if they were pointed. You will feel the stretch on the midline of your left leg as you lift your leg upward. Keep your leg as straight as you can. Move your leg against resistance both directions.

If you have an exaggerated curve in your spine, you can bend the left arm and slide your hand behind the back to keep your awareness there and to encourage it to flatten. If you feel compression in the neck, bring your right arm under your head.

Continue to raise and lower your left leg in sync with your breathing nine times. Feel resistance as you raise and as you lower your leg. Raise your leg with the inhalation and lower it with the exhalation. This stage benefits the prostate gland in men and the reproductive glands of both men and women. The organs of the lower abdomen are strengthened due to a surplus of oxygenated blood and the hip joints become strong. The nerves and muscles of the leg are strengthened.

Now stop the movement and with the leg still lifted roll onto your stomach. Your chin is on the floor. Your arms are alongside of your body. Maintain the stretch through your left leg. The leg is extended and lifted. Hold for several nice long breaths in the spine. You feel support from the pelvic floor muscles, the abdominals tightened at the navel center and your spinal breathing. Lower your left leg to the floor.

Move your left arm away from the body and roll over onto your left side. Flex both feet. Adapt the posture appropriately for you and begin to raise and lower the right leg. Do not roll forward. Your lower leg can be bent for a broader base of support. Your right arm can be folded into the lower back or left arm can be brought under your head to give it better support. The movement of your leg is coordinated with the breath and there is resistance in both directions. Keep the pelvic floor lift and navel tight. Lift and lower nine times.

Stop the movement with the leg lifted and roll onto your stomach. Your chin is on the floor and your arms are alongside of your body. Your right leg is extended and lifted. The increased traction in the spine will free up energy. Do not strain, breathe.

In the third stage your arms rest alongside the body and your chin is on the floor. Stretch your chin forward as you raise both legs upward. Tighten your pelvic floor muscles and pull the navel center toward the spine. Inhale and lift both legs together upward. Lift your thighs as high as you can. The pelvis is pressing against the floor. Hold your legs up for a count of ten, breathing smoothly and evenly. Lower your legs down to the floor and take a deep breath to relax. Again, inhale and lift the legs for a count of ten, remembering to breathe smoothly and evenly. The breath, and the contraction in the pelvic floor and abdomen, add strength and reduce the amount of energy required in this lift. Lower your legs to the floor, and take a breath to relax. For a third and final time, raise your legs. Hold them upward, for as long as you can comfortably.

Release the legs down and relax completely. Turn your head so that your right cheek is on the floor. If your breath has speeded up, slow it down. Don't let your mind wander. Stay focused on the sensations in the body. Release any discomfort with an exhalation. Relax for fifteen to thirty seconds. Turn your head to other side and relax another fifteen to thirty seconds.

Now, bring the hands to shoulder level, and come on to your hands and knees. Shift your weight back bringing your buttocks back toward your heels with your arms extended. Stretch through your arms, from your shoulders. Open your armpits. Your head is in alignment with your spine. Press your toes into the floor. Breathe. Press into your hands and lift your tailbone up, come up onto your toes and shift your weight back. Your chin comes to your chest. Hold the stretch for several breaths, pressing the outside edge of your heels toward the floor. Finally, come up on your toes again and step forward with your right foot, bringing it to your right hand. Step forward with your left foot, bringing it to your left hand. Bring your palms together at your heart center in *vanekom mudra* and roll up to standing, vertebra by vertebra. Your heels come together and your feet separated. Feel relaxation through your legs. Press through the ball and heel of both feet. Your shoulders are open, shoulder blades back and down, and your hands in *vanekom mudra* at the heart center.

Caution: People with heart disease or weaknesses in the heart should avoid the third stage of the posture, or select a variation described below and perform it very slowly. Full Grasshopper places substantial pressure on the heart. With the legs lifted and the head and arms on the floor, there is an increase in chest pressure, which increases the heart rate and heightens the tension in the cervical spine.

Adaptations for Grasshopper:

1) Spread your arms forward and either bring the palms together or keep the arms open, fingers outstretched. Lift your head and both arms, as you lift your legs off the ground.

2) Begin with your arms alongside of your body. Then, with your inhalation, you sweep your arms forward as you lift your legs and head up off the ground. On exhalation you bring your arms back alongside the body as you bring your head and legs down to the floor.

The 15th Asana - *Vajroli Mudrasana*, the Supine Pose of Firmness and Light

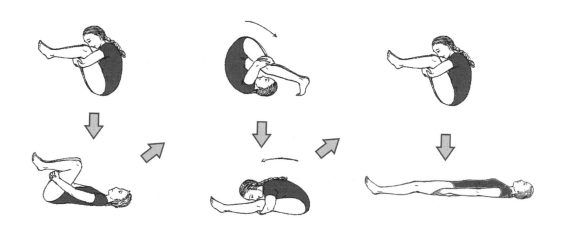

Vajrolimudrasana combines a balancing posture, which stimulates an increase of energy, with a dynamic plough posture, which flushes the circulation system, balances the nerves and distributes that energy throughout the body. The power of digestion and absorption is increased, for the various positions of the body activate the intestinal peristalsis, improving digestion and help with problems of constipation and facilitate the breakdown of fats by exercising the liver and gall bladder. The pelvic region is stretched and blood flow is increased in the intestines and reproductive organs. Circulation to the prostrate, adrenals and kidneys is improved. Swelling in the feet can be relieved.

The balance on the sacrum awakens the dynamic energy at the root *adhara, muladhara* and may stimulate a sustained movement into *svadhisthana,* at the sacrum. The posture can increase the vital energy, making the body feel energized and rather luminous.

****

Sit with your legs bent in toward your chest. Interlace your fingers under the knees, and rock back onto the sacrum lifting your feet. It should be easy to balance on that flat triangular part of the lower spine. Straighten your spine and drop your chin to your chest. Engage your pelvic floor muscles (*mulabandha*) and tighten the navel center. Breathe long, deep *ujjayi* breaths from the *muladhara.* You can straighten your legs upward or keep them bent. Remain focused on spinal breathing with *ujjayi pranayama.*

Can you sense energy rising inside the spinal column? This posture can awaken the central nadi in the spinal cord, the *sushumna*. Keep the pose active with the breath. You can be held effortlessly in this balance, by tightening the pelvic floor and abdominal muscles and by actively utilizing the *prana* through the breathing in the spine. Draw energy up the spine as you inhale and feel it expand as you exhale.

The second stage of the pose is a dynamic plough, which incorporates a plough and a forward fold. Keep the pelvic muscles and navel center tightened and the chin into the chest and your hands under your knees. Inhale and roll backward, bringing your legs over the head, keeping the legs straight and perhaps touching the floor behind you with the toes. Then, exhale and roll up to sitting position and into a forward bend. Lengthen the spine and bend all the way forward, extending your legs fully. Then, inhaling, again roll backward. As you roll backward bring your knees close to the forehead to avoid pressure in the neck. Roll back only onto the shoulders. Do not roll on the neck. Exhale and roll forward. Continue back and forth nine times.

This dynamic posture flows on the breath. The vertebrae open and energy flows through the capillaries and out through the whole of the body. Start slowly. Always keep your body in alignment and stretch out completely both forward and backward. Focus on the *manipura*, (at navel-solar plexus) as you roll from one position to the other. Notice the invigoration this posture stimulates.

The third stage brings you back again to center, balancing again on your sacrum with your hands still interlaced behind your knees. Drop your chin to your chest and again tighten your navel center toward the spine and squeeze your pelvic floor muscles. Keep the knees bent or extend them upwards. Continue spinal breathing. Balanced at the sacrum, imagine yourself centered in the *sushumna nadi*, with energy rising in the spinal column and light forming around the body.

Release your feet to the floor. Bring your hands to your knees and with your abdominal muscles tightened and chin to chest, roll onto your back into *shavasana*. Relax your shoulders, with your arms away from the body, palms up, legs wide apart, and feet turn outward. Turn your head from side to side. Relax. Don't let the mind wander. Keep awareness on the sensations of spaciousness, light, coolness, heat, or vibration in the body. Relax for thirty seconds.

To stretch the spine, bring your legs together and your arms above your head. Point and flex your feet and stretch in both directions. Exhale, with your chin to chest, and abdominals and pelvic floor tightened. Come up to touch your toes. Sit up.

The 16th Asana - *Supta Vajrasana*, the Kneeling Pose of Firmness (counterpose)

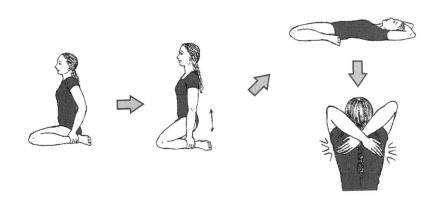

Suptavajrasana, the kneeling pose of firmness, stretches and massages the abdominal organs and aids in alleviating digestive ailments and constipation. It exercises the sacral, lumbar, thoracic and cervical areas of the spine toning the spinal nerves and increases flexibility in the back. The spinal cord, medulla oblongata, cerebellum and cerebrum are positively affected by the backward bend of the upper torso and head. The chest is stretched and expanded to full capacity, bringing more oxygen into the system, so it is especially useful for those with asthma and bronchitis. There is good circulation throughout the sacral areas and pelvic region. The navel center is strengthened, and the pancreas and adrenal glands are toned. The pose can increase healthy secretions of insulin. This pose loosens the legs, knees and ankle, hip and shoulder joints, and strengthens the quadriceps, which helps to support the knees and so prepares the body for sitting for meditation. It can release anxiety and mental tensions stored in the hips and pelvis. Fatty accumulation around the thigh and calf is reduced. It is good for the bones, muscles, nerves and blood vessels of the feet, shins, knees, thigh, abdomen, chest, throat, neck and head. Releasing all the way into the reclining pose relaxes the downward pull of gravity on the cells of the body so that the body receives more energy.

Vajra refers to the nerve and energy pathways that connect the sexual organs to the brain. The *vajra nadi* carries sexual fluid within the subtle body. *Suptavajrasana* increases secretions of the sexual glands. These secretions are very powerful. It is the essence of our dynamic energy. When held for extended lengths of time, *suptavajrasana* reduces heat in the *vajra nadi* and redirects sexual energy. When sexual energy is sublimated and transformed into a fine substance known as *ojas*, creativity is enhanced. This higher vibrational energy will deepen your meditation. Mental clarity is enhanced to help you better adapt to change. The position can improve self-control, quieting the mind and sexual desire.

Suptavajrasana does create pressure in the knee, but it also helps strengthen the quadriceps tendon. The two major muscles of the upper leg, the hamstrings and the quadriceps, cross the knee and help to maintain the integrity of the joint. The knee cap (patella) is surrounded by the quadriceps tendon. Strengthening the quadriceps muscles can help to prevent the patella from dislocating.

****

Kneel down onto your mat. Bring your knees and feet together. Sit back on your heels into *vajrasana*. (You can perform the pose from this position, with the right big toe over the left big toe). However, if your knees are pain-free, spread your feet apart, and gently sit down between your heels. Bring your hands to your thighs or on your ankles. The first stage will strengthen your quadriceps muscles. Using your upper thigh muscles, not your arms, lift and lower your buttocks. Move with the breath, inhaling as you lift your buttocks upward and exhaling as bring your buttocks to the floor. Keep your back straight. Keep your pelvic floor muscles and navel center tightened to support your back. If your ankles are uncomfortable, support them with a folded towel.

There should be no discomfort in your knee. If there is some discomfort, try widening the space between your knees. By rolling the calf muscle out to the side you can make more space to sit comfortably. Make certain that your spine is straight not rounded, the crown of the head is pressing upward. Move slowly and consciously, lifting and releasing your buttocks to the floor. If your buttocks touch the floor easily, and there is no discomfort in your knees, you can chose to pick up speed and bounce your buttocks to the floor for a count of thirty. This will stimulate energy at the base of the spine. Keep your back straight.

To move into *Suptavajrasana*, the second stage, bring your hands back behind you, with fingers facing backward and then lean back onto the support of your hands. Elongate your neck, dropping the back of your head into the support of your shoulders and breathe. Keep a stretch in your thighs and your knees pressed downward. There is a gentle tilt in your pelvis so that your sacrum moves down toward the floor.

If you want a deeper stretch, bring your elbows and forearms to the floor, hands to your feet and take the crown of your head to the floor as in Fish Pose. Keep your knees in contact with the floor. You will feel the stretch in the quadriceps, but don't force the knees straining the muscles and ligaments of the thigh and knee. Keep the pelvic floor muscles (*mulabandha*) and navel center tightened. Begin spinal breathing. This position deeply arches the lower back. This position will deeply stretch the quadriceps and psoas muscles, and stretch and massage the abdominal organs.

Remain here and breathe deeply and smoothly, or drop deeper by sliding the back of your head to the floor. Bring your chin into your chest. Extend your arms above your head. Breathe deeply and consciously bring energy upward in the spine. Keep your knees pressed down toward the floor and your chin to your chest. Keep the *mulabandha* tightened along with the navel center. Sense the deeply relaxing quality of the pose. (For spiritual benefits, you can rest in this pose for longer periods). The breath may become more and more subtle. Relax into the position or come back to a previous stage, if you begin to feel discomfort in your knee.

If you are comfortable, cross your arms behind your head reaching toward the opposite shoulder blade and pat your back thirty times. This can balance the subtle channels, the ida and pingala and stimulate energy flow in points in the upper back. Alternatively, rise back to the position seated between your feet, before you cross your arms behind you to stimulate these points on your back.

To move out of the posture, slowly bring your arm to support your lower back, and lift up one side at a time. Be careful that you do not put too much torque on your knees. Relax the legs out and massage any tension in the knees and pat out both sides of the legs. Lie back into *shavasana* for thirty seconds. Take your head from side to side to release any blocked energy. Stretch out fully through the spine. On an exhalation, come up to touch your toes, with your pelvic floor and navel center tightened, and chin to chest. Sit up. Cross your left leg over your right and come up to standing without the use of your hands, if possible. Your feet are hip distance apart. Bring your heels together, your feet apart. Press through the heel and ball of your foot. Feel relaxation through your legs. Open your shoulders, lift the crown of your head, chin down. Bring hands into *vanekom mudra*. Come to standing.

Caution: Counter-indicated for people with sciatica, slipped disks, sacral conditions or bad knees.

The 17th Asana – *Trikonasana*, the Triangle Pose
(Pose and Counter-pose)

Trikonasana is a triangle pose with ten variations. The counter-poses are included. This powerful series tones the spine as the spinal cord receives a steady pull. The muscles in the front and the back of the body are fully stretched. The side muscles of the torso are also alternately contracted and relaxed and stretched. All the spinal nerves are bathed in a full supply of blood. The hips are given a stretch. The legs, trunk, head, bones of the legs, spine, arms, muscles nerves, ligaments and tendons are stretched along with the glands and blood vessels. Circulation is strengthened. The chest is expanded so that the chambers of the lungs open and oxygen is increased in the blood. The belly is expanded and all of the alimentary canal organs are strengthened. The liver, gallbladder, kidneys, pancreas, adrenal glands, spleen and diaphragm all benefit. Fatty deposits in the abdomen are slowly eliminated.

The quality of the Triangle Pose is strength and the ability to support weight and resist pressure. The Triangle Pose brings the body into balance. In particular, the energy channels (nadis) in the lower back are flushed and strengthened. All the adharas benefit. Concentrate your focus at the navel/solar plexus center in the *manipura* as you move through the series.

****

Standing, take a wide step to the right and to the left. Your feet face straight forward. Your knees are soft. Do not lock out or hyper-extend your knees. Your kneecap should point over the center of the foot. Create a strong foundation. Press down through the heel and ball of both feet. Extend your arms straight out from the shoulders. Relax the shoulder blades down. Point with the index finger and curl the other fingers inside the thumb. This is *anushasan mudra*, which influences the spinal column and brings vitality. It is the mudra for discipline and increases efficiency and success. Lift through the crown of the head. Take long deep ujjayi breaths.

1) Turn and look out over your right arm at your index finger. Continue to hold your gaze on your index finger as you slowly lift your right arm upward and release your left arm downward. Be sure you are using a full stretch through both arms. Bend at the hips. Take your left index finger toward the center of your left great toe. Press into the toenail if you can. Press down equally through both feet. Lengthen through the crown of the head. Energy flows from the center to the periphery of your body. Your head is turned so that your chin is over your right shoulder. Your eyes maintain their gaze at your right index finger. Be careful that you do not strain your neck. (*If there is too much tension in your neck, alternately, turn your head to look down at the left index finger). Breathe deeply with *ujjayi* pranayama, holding the position for at least three breaths.

2) Slowly move your left hand toward your right great toe. Press into the toe if possible. Keep an active lengthening in your arms. Energy flow will increase through your arms, if you use all your muscles from the shoulders to the fingers. Keep the length in the spine and a lifting at the crown of the head. Keep your hips flat, even as you begin to twist deeper, rolling the torso upward toward the right. Take at least three long deep *ujjayi* breaths.

To come out of the position, slowly return your left hand back to the left toe. Extend through both arms, eyes focused on the right index finger. Press down through both feet. Breathe deep into the spine. The breath will support you as your right arm leads you back up to the center position.

3) Slowly turn your head to look at your left index finger. Move your chin directly over your left shoulder. Lift your left arm up. Bend at your hips so that your right hand drops down toward your right great toe. Extend through both arms. Press into the toe nail with your right index finger, if possible. (*There is no need to bend your knees to reach your toe). Continue to look up at the left index finger. (Alternately, turn your head to look at your right index finger). It is important that your legs are as straight as possible without hyperextending your knees and that you press equally through both feet. You will feel muscular lengthening through the arms and through the spine. Take at least three long, deep breaths.

4) Slowly move the right hand to the left great toe. Allow your chest to rotate toward the left, while keeping your hips flat. Take at least three long *ujjayi* breaths. Breathing should be smooth and relaxed. If you experience tension, try exhaling out through your mouth. If you extend your inhalation you will increase strength to the body. Extending your exhalation better releases tension or discomfort. To come out of the pose, return your right finger back to your right great toe. Take a deep spinal breath. Allow the left arm to lift your body back to center. Breathe. You will experience an increasing flow of energy.

*If your back is tight, you may not be able to touch your toes. Even if you can only bend from the waist you will still benefit from the stretch. Do try to keep your legs straight, but avoid hyperextension of the knees. You can protect your knees by pressing through both the eel and ball of both feet in every position.

5) Squeeze your pelvic floor muscles (*mulabandha*) and tighten your navel center to support your lumbar spine in this next position. These contraction along with the stretch through your arms and legs and the spinal breathing will internally support the pose by increasing energy in the subtle channels and bring a sense of vitality and relaxation to the body and mind. The Ujjayi breathing will direct new circulation of oxygenated blood throughout the spinal nerves, increasing blood flow into the thyroid, parathyroid and the brain.

Extend your arms fully from the shoulder as you **bend forward, moving from the hips**. Your feet are still facing forward. You are pressing though both the heel and ball of your feet. Your head and neck are relaxed. Bend forward until you feel a tightening in the musculature, then pause and begin the kriyas. These pulsing movements will release deep muscle tension, relaxing you into the stretch.

6) Press into both feet equally and using the pelvic floor and abdominal muscles for support, **come upright, on one inhalation**. Hold at the center position, for at least one deep breath before releasing backward. Your arms remain extended out from the shoulder. Lift your chest and chin. The arch in the thoracic spine comes from the lift of the chest and chin. Your upper back will gently arch, as your lower back stretches. Press your pelvis forward as a counterweight. Feel the upper back supported as you move into this

gentle backbend. Do not compress the lumbar spine. Be aware of the smooth even flow of your breath as you relax backward. If you find you are holding your breath, you are arching too deeply. A secret to developing this pose is to maintain an even breathing pattern. If breathing becomes difficult or restricted, slowly straighten back to center and begin again.

*The *ujjayi* spinal breathing and body awareness will support you, as you ease into the backbend and lift back to center. Stay aware of your body as it moves in space. Maintain the *mulabandha* (pelvic floor muscles squeezed) and the tightened navel center. Consciously lift again from your chest and chin to return to the center. You will experience support from the lines of energy flowing from the navel up the spine toward your head and out through your extended arms.

7) In this next variation, be sure that your feet remain in the same forward position. Do not rotate them to the right side. Keeping your feet forward will assure you a "good stretch" in the hips, knees and ankles. Keep your arms fully extended. Slowly **rotate your torso and arms to face the right side.** Your feet must stay flat on the floor. If the inside edge of your right foot lifts up, you have rotated too far to the right. Release the rotation, until the foot returns back to the floor. Tighten the pelvic floor muscles and your navel center. Contract your right thigh. Lift your right femur up into the hip joint. **Bend at the hip, over your right leg**. Bring your face toward your right knee. Pause when you feel the musculature tighten and begin the kriyas, pulsing gently into the stretch several times. Don't bounce to force the stretch. The movements help to release and relax you. Relax your neck and head. You may feel a bit of torque at the ankles, knees and hips. This should feel good. Breathe deeply. Enjoy the stretch.

8) Pressing into both feet, and extending through your arms, raise your torso up on one inhalation, facing right. Pause, when your torso is upright and take a breath (otherwise you can become light-headed). Then, lift your chest and chin and **release backward** arching your back gently. Keep lengthening through both arms and pressing through both feet. Don't bend your knees. Lift your chest and chin and open your heart and throat. Take several breaths. Inhale and come back upright, still facing right.

9) **Rotate your torso to the left**. Don't over rotate. If the inside of your left foot lifts up off the floor, release the rotation a bit. Press down into both feet and bend forward slowly at the hips. Contract your left thigh, lifting the femur up into the hip socket and **release your torso** over your left leg. Stop when you feel the muscles tighten and begin the kriya movements. Relax into the stretch, bringing your nose as close to the knee as possible and breathe, letting go into the stretch.

10) Keep the pelvic floor and navel center tightened. Keep your arms extended. Inhale and press through both feet as you raise your torso back upright. Pause and take a breath. Then, lift your chest and chin and **release backward**. Feel the space of the heart and throat

open. Stay tuned to the quality of the breath. If you find that you are holding your breath, you are working too hard. As you relax into the posture, your breath will flow effortlessly. You will feel completely supported. Stay lifted in the chest and the chin as you slowly rise back up, still facing left.

Turn your body **back to center**. Bend your right knee slightly and push off your right foot, bringing your right foot to meet your left. Bring your hands together at the heart in *vanekom mudra*, drawing the energy from the periphery into the center. Be aware of the changing sensations in your spine and in your breath and in the space around your body. Take at least thirty seconds as you rest, standing in stillness. Joy arises when we create space in the body and fill it with prana and consciousness.

The 18th Asana - *Purna Shanti Shavasana*, **Complete Peace and Relaxation Pose**

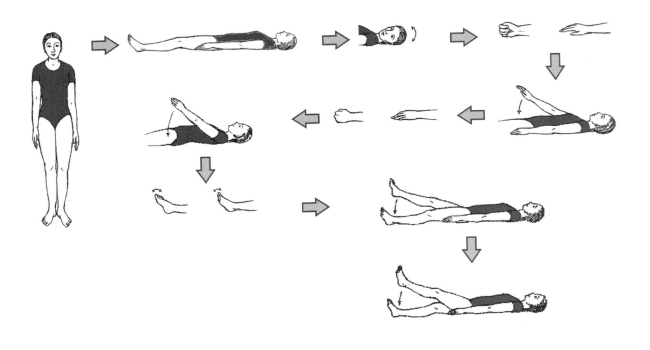

This *shavasana* (corpse pose) series systematically relaxes the whole of the body and mind. It removes the effects of stress from the skeleton, the muscles, the tissues and the cells, relaxing every tissue in the body. It is a relaxation technique of contraction and release. It is an excellent relaxation technique especially for beginners. It provides a systematic way of learning how to relax the different parts of the body through exaggerating the tension and then releasing it. It is through consciously creating tension in the muscles that we can acknowledge the feeling of tension. When release immediately follows the tension, the feeling of relaxation is unmistakable.

Shavasana will promote blood circulation throughout the body and produce relaxation in every tissue. Practiced regularly one will experience pulsing energy, warmth, relief of fatigue and a deep sense of peace. The nervous system is toned and mental clarity is increased as blood pressure is reduced. The *shavasana* is often used as treatment for many diseases and is a key to strengthening the cardio-vascular system.

When the body is totally still, the mind will bring forth all kinds of things, random and unexpected, or ordinary or extraordinary thoughts. Regardless of what comes up, keep a sense of distance between who you are and these thoughts. By observing breathing and chanting the words for peace and God at the end of the *shavasana*, a message of deepest relaxation and peace is sent to all levels of your being.

Although *Shavasana* is simple to practice it is most difficult to master. Mastery requires bringing peace to all levels of your being. Babaji says, first, bring peace to all levels of your being, and then share that peace and joy with others. This is to realize the goal of Babaji's Kriya Yoga: The universal vision of Love.

****

Lie down on your back. Open your legs wide with your feet supinated (rolled open to the side). Align yourself head, neck and spine. *You can choose to support your back by placing a cushion or rolled blanket under your knees. Move your arms away from the body with the palms upward. Feel the pull of gravity, the sense of heaviness of where the body touches the floor.

Bring your **awareness** to the head and neck. **Release your head very slowly from side to side, so slowly that you feel** every movement-in-space. Keep your attention on the sensations in the head and neck and release any residual tension or blocked energy in the throat. Then, rock your head back to center.

Bring your attention down into your right hand. Spread and stretch your fingers and bring the thumb into the center of the palm and make a fist. Squeeze your fist as tight as you can. Keep focused and breathe energy down into your hand. Then let go, and with the hand relaxed slowly bring your forearm up to the elbow and let it drop. Then lift your whole right arm a few inches, and let it go. Notice the difference between your right arm and your left. Take your awareness into the left hand. Spread and stretch out through your fingers, and bring the thumb into the palm and make a fist. Tighten it more and release it. Then with the hand relaxed, lift your forearm up to the elbow and let it drop. Then, lift your whole arm up a few inches and let it go. Bring your awareness to the right foot. Stretch out the toes, spread them and move them forward and back several times, and release them. Then direct your awareness to the toes of the left foot. Spread the toes of the left foot. Feel the space between the toes, and release them. Rotate the feet inward and outward, feeling the rotation all the way into the hips. Notice how heavy your legs are as you lift them, one at a time, a couple of inches and let them drop back to the floor.

The physical body will experience a deep level of relaxation and a sense of increased inner space. However, the mind may still be dispersed and run in many directions. The subconscious may bring up random, and unexpected, thoughts. To allow the deep sense of relaxation and peace to penetrate the mind, chant the Shanti Mantra. The mantra will create a relaxation response and a sense of peace and detachment from any thought that may arise.

The sounds in this mantra, all reflect the qualities of peace and God in various traditions around the world. They resonate with our inner energies, and unfold in us the pure meaning behind the sounds. The sounds stimulate vibration, light and harmony in the cells of our being. Chanting aloud with others enhances the experience. By both chanting and listening to the resonating voices the mind begins to identify with an experience of Consciousness and Peace shared by us all.

Chant the first *shanti* boldly for world peace, the second *shanti* softer, for family, friends, neigborhood and the third *shanti* still softer, for your own individual peace.

Om, Shanti, Shanti, Shanti, Shalom, Sat Nam, Sadhu, Tao, Em, Aum, Spirit, Swami, Kami, Amin, Amen, Aumen, Selah, Hum, Aum

For one minute… **Just be still**.

Chapter 4

Babaji's Kriya Yoga Sadhana — The Importance of an Integral, Fivefold Path

The *sadhana* (discipline) of Babaji's Kriya Yoga is an integrated fivefold path to awareness. That is to say, each limb incorporates awareness into the practice of asana, pranayama, meditation, mantra and devotion, and that the individual practices contain all five limbs within it. The asana practice includes elements of pranayama, meditation, mantra and devotion, just as every other single practice, incorporates all five limbs. It is precisely because Kriya Yoga is such an integrated *sadhana* that it has enormous potential to make one a more conscious human being.

The word *sadhana* comes from the Sanskrit root, *saad*, meaning "to go straight to a goal; to accomplish; to master." *Sadhana* indicates a daily disciplined practice of yogic techniques. All the Kriya techniques teach one how to reach a state of awareness. The goal is to be witness to life's experiences, moment to moment, and in so doing incorporate awareness in all thoughts, words, dreams, desires and actions. In a nutshell, all you do to uncover your true Self and all you do to let go of what obscures its true nature, is the Kriya Yoga *sadhana*. It is a way of being, seeing and living, which shifts your sense of "I am" away from its identification with the body, thoughts, emotions and personal history. As a result, awareness develops and the true "I" is revealed.

Babaji's Kriya Yoga is a progressive system of exercises and spiritual practices for integrated self-development. Kriya Yoga *sadhana* comprises all the parts of your being and will work through all the activities of your being, and thus can literally change your outer nature. It can change what you are doing in life and even what you thought yourself capable of doing. It actualizes your potential. It is dynamic and transformational Yoga, which enables the mastery of your life and karma so you can discover your dharma.

Yoga explains that karma lies behind whatever happens in our life. Every situation is a reflection of our karma—cause and effect, every action having a corresponding and equal reaction. Each personality is a mass of *samskaras*, mostly unconscious impressions and tendencies. These *samskaras* stimulate habitual thinking, speaking and acting, which influence our karma. What happens in our life, the quality of birth, lifespan and life experiences are determined by our combined karmas. While a very strong karma from the past brings certain situations into our present life, how we choose to handle each situation can affect our karma in the future. Karmas can be changed through awareness of our tendencies, if we are willing to eliminate those which cause attachment and suffering. By using discrimination and willpower, we can learn to replace ego-centric habits and reactions with actions that edify others and bring detachment and equanimity to our self. In this way we can come to terms with our karma as it is and be at peace.

Karmic impressions exist in all five bodies and the five bodies interpenetrate one another. Emotions arise in and affect the vital body. However, habitual agitation from frustration, anger, fear, greed, pride or envy can cause disease in the physical and mental body. Disease can develop in the physical body when there is disharmony in the spiritual. Also anything that feeds the physical, vital, mental, and/or intellectual bodies will have a direct affect on the spiritual body.

Yoga is a means of developing all five bodies together, in a peaceful and harmonious manner. This is what is referred to as integration of the five bodies. It is not enough to simply develop physically through Hatha Yoga, or only spiritually through Bhakti Yoga. Full integration requires preparation on all levels of one's being. Babaji's Kriya prepares the entire being. The various techniques work with synergy on the defects of the physical and mental and the shortcomings of the emotional, intellectual and spiritual bodies. For example, the practice of the **asana** not only purifies the physical, but also leaves the mind and emotions in a calm state. The practice of **pranayama** purifies both the physical body, releasing physical toxins and the vital body, releasing difficult emotions. Pranayama and mudra connect mind and life energy (*prana*), which direct vital life energy within the subtle nadis, energizes the physical body, sharpening the intellect and opening one to subtle sight. The practice of **meditation** can release the effects of stress on the physical body, soothe the mind and sharpen the intellect and open one to a flow of intuition. The practice of **mantra japa** (repetition) suspends habitual thoughts and unravels the threads of the mind, creating space for inspiration and insight to descend from a higher intelligence. In addition, repeating mantra has been shown to strengthen the physical organ systems and enhance willpower and one's ability to discriminate. The techniques of **devotion** create the magic to invoke grace, and instill Truth in the heart and mind. In other words, devotion creates the temple in which the other bodies dwell. It creates the foundation necessary for the other techniques to be successful and the goal to be reached. Contentment, joy or bliss experienced in the spiritual body will profoundly affect the other four.

The potency of each particular practice will vary from person to person. This is because we are not all integrated to the same extent. Full integration requires participation with awareness on all levels of one's being. Rare is the person who participates with all of his/her being, doing anything. Babaji's Kriya Yoga can prepare the entire being for self realization, but for most people it takes consistency, over time. One will begin to experience better health and more energy, and then mental clarity and a more balanced emotional nature. Later, there is heightening of the physical and subtle senses and a widening of perspective that is less self-centered and more compassionate. Such transformation is possible for anyone who commits to a regular, daily Kriya Yoga practice.

Kriya Kundalini Pranayama —
The Scientific Art of Mastering the Breath and Mind

Kriya Kundalini Pranayama is the most potent technique in Babaji's Kriya Yoga. Pranayama is heralded by the Siddhas as a means to longevity. The Siddhas say that man's normal life span is one hundred years, but that it is irregularities in breathing, due to habitually poor living habits, which result in a premature deterioration of the systems of the body. Thus, it is rare for a person to actually live to be one hundred. The objective of pranayama is to correct irregular breathing and the bad habits that cause it. Kriya Kundalini Pranayama slows, deepens and regulates the breath and various physical systems. It is an elegant and powerful technique that increases, extends and directs subtle life energy into the physical body. It brings strength and homeostasis to the physical nervous system, while it purifies, regulates and circulates increased amounts of vital life energy (*prana*) throughout the tissues of the body.

In Sanskrit, *Pran-ayama* means (first unit of energy)-(extender). The word is composed of sounds that carry the meaning, "to breathe with that, which is eternal." This is because *prana* is cosmic energy and the subtle vital energy of life. It is dynamic energy, both physical and mental. It is pure energy and not oxygen, nor glycogen. It is not a gas. It is more subtle. It is the energy of life, that numinous substance that is the form of the all-pervasive energy in the Universe. It is truly one's source of power, enthusiasm and effective dynamism. It is a vital energy field of sexual energy, psychic energy, dynamic energy, essential energy for all function of the living beings (bioplasm).

Prana is widely available to everyone. *Prana* is in the atmosphere. It is taken into the body through the breath, but it is also absorbed from sunlight, and through eating fresh prana-rich foods and drinking prana-rich water and increased through meditation. With some practice, *prana* globules can even be seen floating in the atmosphere due to their brilliance and vibration. *Prana* is pouring forth continually from the sun. It is not a force of light, but it does depend upon light for manifestation.

When *prana* enters through respiration it becomes divided into five kinds of energy with specific functions. *Prana* function relates to respiration, *samana* to digestion, *apana* to elimination, *vyana* to physical coordination, and *udana* to integration. These five functions must be balanced. An imbalance in one will create disturbances in the others. Disease and aging are said to be reactions to low or imbalanced pranic levels. Regular practice of pranayama is imperative if decay of the physical body is to be overcome.

The Siddhas refer to *prana* as the "intelligence" that animates and breathes the body. They say that it is the *prana* that draws in each inhalation and expels each exhalation. It is the "fire" working in the lungs and the heart and converting oxygen into an internal force of vitality. It is this force, which connects with blood and oxygenates it, gives blood its red color, and circulates it throughout the body. *Prana* vitalizes the individual atoms and cells and supplies electrical force to the nerves. It magnetizes the iron in the system and produces a natural emanation around the body (aura). The aura becomes a strong magnetic force and a reservoir of energy.

Prana is intimately related to the mind and mental processes. Yoga says that *prana* and mind are not structurally different from one another. It is the movement of *prana* in the breath which enables the mind to think. Were it not for the movement of *prana* in the appropriate channels in the body, there would be no movement of the mind to comprehend it. *Prana* moves through the body due to actions, the root of which is the mind. It is due to the movement of *prana* alone that the mind arises. Every thought, which passes through the mind, passes through the body. The breath is the channel that carries these thoughts. Any disturbance in the mind will agitate *prana* in the body. Agitation in the prana will create restlessness in mind. Consistent agitation in either body or mind causes dis-ease within the other. If the breath is slowed down and regulated, the mind will lose its "fuel" to agitate the *prana*. When restlessness in the *prana* subsides, the mind becomes calm.

The "quantity" of one's *prana* is indicated by personal power, enthusiasm, and effective dynamism, but its "quality" is dominated by the personality, by desires, feelings, and passions. Someone may possess abundant *prana* and be powerful, but that power can be of a high or a low vibration, due to his/her thoughts and desires. With regular practice of Kriya Kundalini Pranayama and meditation, the *prana* becomes harmonized and of a higher vibration, so that external disturbances and distractions of the world lose their dominant influence. One develops a deeper and wider perspective and begins to respond differently to events in life. Compassion, acceptance and detachment replace judgment, attachment and frustration. Rather than losing one's temper at the mundane problems of the world, one sees ways of solving them. This is because pranayama is also a process of awareness training.

Kriya Kundalini Pranayama begins the process of "awareness training." Pranayama always involves awareness; otherwise it is just a breathing exercise. Awareness begins with attention. Attention brings the conscious brain into action; however, awareness demands that all of one's attention is focused on one thing. One is one hundred percent involved. Normally, only a small portion of one's attention is concentrated at any one point. Our mind is rarely concentrated on only one thing at a time. We are a multi-tasking people and used to splitting our attention in various directions.

Kriya Kundalini Pranayama does not allow one to multi-task. It creates a natural *pratyahara* (withdrawal of the senses) and *dharana* (one-pointed concentration), which leads to *dhyana* (meditation). If the Kriya pranayamas are practiced, twice a day, with full awareness of what is happening, they will eventually balance the flow of the breath through both nostrils and the subtle nervous system, within the *ida and pingala nadis*. As the outgoing and ingoing breaths become harmonized, *prana* connects with the mind, and one experiences mental steadiness and calm. Thoughts and consciousness become fixed and one is enveloped in lightness, expansion, ascension. The subtle central channel in the spine (*sushumna*) opens, stimulating the flow of a higher vibrational power and consciousness and awakens the subtle energy centers. The process is a gentle awakening of *kundalini shakti*. The energy is directed upward in *sushumna* and eventually penetrates the six principal adharas to reach *sahasrara chakra*, the thousand-petalled lotus at the crown of the head. The corresponding psychological states of each adhara are awakened in this process, along with a new sense of dynamism on all five planes of existence. Once *anahata*, at the heart is pierced and awakened, one begins their journey beyond the normal range of consciousness and towards an inner vision of their true Self.

Babaji's Kriya Yoga Dhyanas — The Scientific Art of Mastering the Mind and Co-creating Your Life

Kriya Yoga *dhyanas* (meditations) are unique. They develop in a progressive series; each meditation builds on the other and helps to develop another level of consciousness. They lead you to inquire into and duly affect all your five bodies. They affect different levels of consciousness: the subconscious and unconscious mind, the intellect and even super-consciousness. They take you through a process where you are encouraged to become consciously aware of your mental conditioning, your desires, aversions and cravings, and then, to consciously abandon them. Kriya meditations work to develop your inner sensing and open up your intuition. They explore the witnessing mind. Witness consciousness is developed during your sessions of meditation, as you experience your center and become aware that you are observing your thoughts. You begin to watch yourself acting, thinking, feeling, hearing, tasting, touching and smelling. This witnessing will eventually continue in your daily routines and guide you in your actions and responses in daily activities and sometimes even during periods of sleep.

The practice of Kriya Dhyana Yoga encourages the truth realized in meditation to penetrate to waking consciousness and become effective there. Used to purify the subconscious, the meditations help to replace habitual false thinking and acting with constructive movements and actions. Guided by a growing awareness in all activities, one becomes attentive, moment to moment. One learns to discriminate and to detach from the useless and negative thoughts that arise to obstruct peace and happiness.

It is how conscious and aware you are, which determines the nature and quality of the life you live. So, rather than trying to stop thoughts and drop into a dreamy space, these meditations focus on dynamic methods to strengthen the power of the mind. They stimulate a ready flow of intuition, inspiration and moment-to-moment awareness applicable to life's challenges and mission.

The Kriya meditations create a discipline to regularly develop and utilize imagination in a creative manner. Man is very creative. Theosophy tells us, "as a man thinks, so he becomes."

We can create out of nothing the things we imagine. We all have a potential for great imagination and powerful projection. Imagination can direct our life. Imagination is the capacity to project oneself outside of realized things and toward things that are realizable, and then draw them to us, through projection. These dhyanas develop and direct that great power of imagination to affect change in our life.

Ordinarily we use our power of imagination inappropriately, for instance through fear, imagining the worst that could happen or judgment, imagining the worst about others, based on limited information. We also misuse our powers of imagination through desire and aversion. We fantasize about how good something would be or we imagine how bad something might become. And, we worry, which amounts to meditating on what we don't want. Kriya Yoga says why not imagine the most positive and constructive things in life? Why imagine catastrophes, when you could just as well imagine positive and healthy outcomes in life? Obviously, imagination is an instrument that must be disciplined.

Imaginations that are built up realistically and consistently with detail and aspiration have a tendency to come about. When we add vital life energy to the process it can become a living force. Most of our imaginings are not very steady and do not have vital life energy behind them, because we usually lose interest and move on to imagine something else. The Kriya Dhyanas provide the discipline required to direct and reorient imagination toward the goals of life. Several of the meditations specifically develop our imagination and visualization in order to create a new reality.

Ultimately, the goal of the advanced Kriya Dhyanas is to reach unity and alignment with the Supreme and its Will, becoming a co-creator in our life. However, this is not possible as long as the ego-motivated preferences are still in play. A variety of meditation techniques offer us an opportunity to remove ego-desires by becoming aware of them, and sometimes playing them out, but also by becoming aware of the aspiration of our soul. These meditations lead us to an awareness of our true self, and help us to discover our dharma and the part we came to play. We begin to understand that we are a part of something much larger than ourselves.

Kriya Dhyanas take us into the deepest states of mental Silence, where there is only awareness. This is the state of *Samadhi*, where the meditator and the meditation merge. In this state, we receive inspiration (*prajna*) from creative consciousness, which then directs our life energy (prana) in all of its activities, including our work, our relationships, and our creative expression.

Kriya Mantra Yoga —
Scientific art of Mastering the Intellect

We are all quite aware of the power of words. Whether we are speaking or thinking them, the words we use affect not only others, but also ourselves. We must choose our words wisely.

Words of anger make us angrier, words of fear make us more fearful and words of love make us more loving. A negative thought or fear can only live on the energy we feed it. Normally we either engage it, or we suppress it. Either way we've fed it. By identifying with it, it remains in our mind and psyche. Repeating the same thoughts or words over and over affect us on deeper and deeper levels. For good or bad, it will carry the message deeper within our subconscious and even into the cells of our physical body.

The mantras used in Kriya Yoga protect the mind from imperfections of ordinary thinking, by moving attention away from any agitation. In his tome, *The Thirumandiram*, Thirumular says it this way, "a mantra saves the one who reflects." Instead of being absorbed in thoughts and impulses that manifest as desires, aversions, emotions and ruminations, one is relieved of them, by repeating a mantra. Even strong emotions like hatred can be neutralized with the right mantra.

A neutral or detached mental state is necessary if you are to effectively cleanse your mind of negative patterns lodged in your subconscious. By combining potent mantra with the rhythm of the breath, you can gain access to the subconscious as well as conscious mind and dislodge even deeply held patterns of hate, fear, anger or sorrow. If you regularly perform *japa* (mantra repetition) your mind becomes disinterested and detached.

When conditioned negative thoughts, emotions or impulses move through the space of your mind, replace them with a mantra instead of engaging them. They will immediately disappear. The proper use of a mantra cools and calms your whole being and turns consciousness toward your soul. Dispassion develops to soothe the passions of the ego. Mantra is not just a combination of letters, syllables or words to uplift the vital body; they are specific vibrations that contain a power to recreate you anew.

How do Mantra's Work on Us?

Yoga science tells us everything is essentially vibration as sound, right down to the atomic level. Sound is the basic creative potential of our being. These sound vibrations revealed themselves within the pure consciousness of Enlightened Siddhas in deepest states of meditation. This essential vibration (*spanda*) is true mantra. Mantra is made up of specific potent sounds or *bijas* (seed syllables). *Bija*-mantra is said to be the microcosmic sound representation of the macrocosmic essence. When the *bija* sound is emitted, this smallest sound unit carries pranic force, which is concentrated at one single point.

The Siddhas used mantra as Holy formulas to reach the Divine. There are *bija* mantras that arise out of the *adharas*. The Siddhas tell us that indeed, *om, na, mah, si, v, ya* arouse from them. *Om* or *lam* arises from muladhara; *na* or *vam* from svadhisthana; *mah* or *ram* from manipura; *si* or *yam* from anahata; *va* or *ham* from vishuddhi; *ya* or *om* from ajna. Different mantras reflect various states of consciousness.

These mantras in Babaji's Kriya Yoga are received and empowered in sacred mantra initiations (*diksha*). These *mantras* are concentrated seeds of purified energy that arouse out of sound radiating power. They are subtle, luminous sounds inaccessible to the external senses. By regularly chanting the mantra silently (*japa*), a person develops an inner calmness and strength, support in his/her yogic sadhana and a capacity to maintain their Kriya discipline. As one continues to repeat the mantra silently it becomes more refined and moves on deeper levels. One experiences the energy intrinsic to each syllable as vibration within the body when one's kundalini assimilates its essence. The vibration, which is created from these sounds, mingles with *prana* to purify the mind and intellect. This is what Yoga means when it says that mantras connect the pulsations of the universe to the root of the mind. The mind is expanded, opening itself to the illumination of the sound itself. At this deeper level we cultivate divine qualities, such as love, compassion, truthfulness, kindness, insightfulness, beauty, discipline, and endurance. The mantra's vibration reaches the soul of a prepared initiate and stimulates the awakening of those qualities within it. Through proper daily *japa*, one begins to choose to identify with the infinite aspects of the soul, rather than with the fleeting demands and aversions of the ego.

Through constant repetition of the names of the Lord, we become capable of experiencing the Presence of the Lord as the divine quality, Love. "Love is manifest where there is an able vessel." (*Narada Bhakti Sutras*) Mantras mold us into vessels capable of manifesting and maintaining divine love. The Siddhas prefer the name *Ishvara* for the name of God, for it has no limiting qualities. *Ishvara* is a composite of two words, "*Shiva*," meaning "the Lord", and "*svara*", which means "one's own true Self." Mantras lead us to experience *Ishvara*, that which is omnipresent, the essential Being behind all names and forms. The names of various deities are reflections of the sounds that reflect certain force and/or qualities of the one Supreme Soul.

The mantras of Kriya Yoga have the potency to take the mind into pure "I" awareness. The mind becomes fixed on the vibration of the mantra and begins to vibrate in tune with it. The individual soul and the pulsation of the Supreme Soul ultimately vibrate in harmony. However, as long as there is the mantra and the one repeating the mantra, duality remains.

Kriya Bhakti Yoga— Developing Love and Finding Truth

Bhakti Yoga is the cultivation of aspiration for God, the Lord as Love or formless Truth. The goal of Kriya Bhakti Yoga is liberation from the limitation of ego identification, of sense-desires and attachment. It is our sense-desires and attachment that lead us on the path of pain and suffering. Ultimately, the Lord as Love is required, in order to root out lust, anger, pride, envy and desire. Only then can we gain freedom from pain and appreciate the joys of life. Chanting, singing, dancing, weeping, praying to God - all these are vital activities, which engage the whole being and invoke Love. However, Kriya Bhakti Yoga suggests invoking the "grace" of Love into each and every Kriya practice, even in asana, pranayama, meditation or mantra.

Bhakti is an activity that feeds an internal fire, which fuels aspiration for the Lord as Love, as it purifies the ego.

Years ago, on a beach in Rishikesh, India, I was shaken out of meditation by the shouts of a sadhu who was acting quite mad. He appeared out of nowhere or so it seemed, in a storm of rants and raves. I opened my eyes to see him swinging a sharp metal sword, storming back and forth across the sands screaming in Hindi or Sanskrit, a language I did not understand. He seemed quite disturbed, even furious. I did not know if he was chanting or angry at all the westerners on the beach or with God Himself. He continued his ranting for most of an hour. The westerners, frightened by his tirade, grabbed their Yoga mats and meditation cushions and scrambled up the rocky coast to find the peace of their hotel gardens. The sadhu continued his rant. I closed my eyes and continue to meditate. I found the sound of his voice authentic, exciting and soothing at the same time. When later, I opened my eyes, the sadhu was sitting next to me, smiling quite sweetly. He spoke in English. " God is Love. Love is God. Sometimes we must demand His attention." The sadhu gave me a clove of garlic and a handful of herbs and told me to eat them, right then and there. I did. Then he said, "never forget that there is no difference between Love and God. To find one, seek out the other."

Any spiritual practice without true love and devotion tends to encourage egoistic tendencies. It is Bhakti, love that develops the steadfastness and firm ground required to control the senses, through which the ego's desires and aversions arise. Kriya Yoga demands that one become aware of the desires and aversions of the ego and learn to control them. But without this last step of expressing Divine love and compassion, the true Self and nature, which is egoless love and compassion, can never be realized.

Devotional activities include kirtan (chanting), personal worship or group rituals, but any gesture done with love, in contemplation of the Divine, even demanding God's attention is a means of devotion. According to the *Bhagavad Gita*, all that is given freely and selflessly without seeking anything in return is devotion. Devotion kept quietly in the heart, yet demonstrated in a life of service, is a powerful means of purification. The activities are not in and of themselves important. Karma Yoga, or selfless service, is the form of Bhakti Yoga most highly respected by Babaji and the Siddhas. What is critical to progress in Babaji's Bhakti Yoga is the experience of uniting with and serving the Truth within and without.

Mantra repetition (*japa*), meditation and compassionate service, along with worship and devotion, are forms of Kriya Bhakti Yoga. Even our asana and pranayama practice can become a form of ritual worship and all of these can have transformational power for one who has love, purity, humility and a one-pointed mind. Kriya Yoga yields transformative power as it helps us discover love in our own heart and stabilize it in our asana, pranayama, mantra, meditation, worship and service.

Devotion is intrinsic to the soul. When a ray of the soul reaches the surface of our external being we glimpse that devotion. It is experienced as causeless joy or love, and we become aware of the vast divinity around us. Bhakti is a means of uncovering and developing the devotional nature of the soul. It is another way to freedom from conditioning and ultimately to transformation. Transformation comes naturally to anyone who is open to the immense power in devotion.

Devotion will open you to the descent of grace. Years of purification are required in order to develop the intense devotion necessary to fully purify and sanctify your thoughts. However, true devotion can draw the grace required to consecrate all your thoughts, in a moment. Through devotion the mind can become so absorbed in the pure emotion of love that it is drawn into *Bhava Samadhi*, which can be described inadequately as complete identification with love itself. Filled with pure sensation of Love, the body is forgotten along with the world. The mind is wholly absorbed in the Beloved. One begins to meditate on the Lord with eyes closed to the world, and to see the Lord with eyes open in the world, foregoing years of Yogic practices. This leads to equanimity, equality, compassion, self-giving and to a spirit of worship in all one sees, thinks and experiences. Such is the power of a devotional heart.

Bhakti is surely a soul-stirring means of understanding certain Spiritual Truths: *we need to possess nothing; we need to be a witness to everything; we are beads strung on the thread that is the Lord Himself, and that thread never breaks and we are never scattered. We see that the Divine holds in His hands all that we are and all that we think we possess and all that we do.*

Progress in Kriya Yoga requires Self-study

The awakening soul has influenced you to take up the spiritual path. It initiated the process when you began to question and feel dissatisfaction with worldly life, regardless of how well it appeared to be going. Questions arose of an existential nature. Life got uncomfortable. Your inner being was pressuring you to wake up. You began to read psychology, philosophy or study scriptures in response to a feeling that something was not right or that something was missing in your life.

The mind and ego need explanations for everything, especially with regard to the awakening of the soul. Any explanation is useful only if the knowledge gleaned, grants true understanding and empowerment, which continues to advance the soul. Spiritual Progress requires some agreement between the mind and the ego. Therefore whole being must be initiated into a path to establish the governance of the soul towards transformation. Kriya Yoga offers initiations that both empowers the breath and gives techniques to concentrate the mind to ensure one hundred percent participation in that pursuit.

However, for progress on the path you need to move beyond the ego. This demands constant self study. Self-study, or *swadhayaya*, is not just study of sacred texts it also includes remembering "who am I" and seeing clearly what you are not: the body, emotions, the mental movements of desire and aversion. The latter are vehicles that the ego uses to travel through time and space in this world, bumping up against your karma and your nature of restlessness and inertia. It is by seeing the interplay of all of these, clearly, which liberates the true "Self" or soul, or Witness consciousness from egoism.

To awake to the soul fully, the mind must shut off the influence of the ego. The mind and ego are strong and often conniving, so a concentrated daily practice of purification must be undertaken to rid oneself of weaknesses, shortcomings, and passions. The ego can be deceptive and seduce one to believe that thoughts and impulses are arriving out of great spiritual light, when more often this is not the case. All thoughts, feelings and actions must be vigilantly observed, and all thoughts and actions that arise in error or from misguidance must be acknowledged and corrected. Although ego-centric mistakes are not easily recognizable, the qualities of balance, mental peace and inner prosperity are recognizable for one in accord with the soul.

Confusion, anger, insincerity, hatred, jealousy and selfishness will repel your soul's influence. Conflicting emotions will limit the influence of your soul in the higher centers. Your *samskaras* (subconscious habitual ways of thinking and acting) will arise repeatedly with stronger and stronger force until you are able to see them as habitual impulses and mechanical habits. You must confront them, to reduce egoism. You will not experience equanimity as a natural result of *sadhana* if you do not. It is not enough to only have upward opening and experiences acquired in deep states of meditation. Kriya Yoga demands that you integrate a widening of higher consciousness into all levels of your being and activities of your life.

As you aspire and allow for your individualized soul to manifest more and more in your life, the qualities of the soul - purity, harmony, beauty, joy and truth - will spontaneously arise. As you create a vital and mental environment conducive to the soul's influence, equanimity will dawn in the mind and heart. Qualities of the soul cannot be taught or practiced; they come about naturally as you align your physical, vital and mental bodies with the soul. By being inwardly calm and absolutely sincere in your actions, you bring your inner being to the forefront.

Subtle changes in your life, and in the way you feel and in what you know and also in how you respond, will make you aware that the soul is stepping up its influence. With the soul's influence, *karma* is often worked out in interesting, dramatic or new ways. Your *dharma* is recognized as a totality of your spirit begins to express itself by embracing your universality, your world and the beings in it.

Your Life Becomes Your Yoga

A disciplined, integrated daily practice of asana, pranayama, mantra, meditation and devotion will create the internal heat necessary to raise your energy and consciousness to such a degree that you begin to see from a new perspective. More and more you will find that you choose to be the Witness to the drama of your life. Witnessing frees you from conditioning. You no longer identify with the patterns the mind and body has established relating to its likes and dislikes, its aversions and desires, its discomfort and pleasure. By repeatedly observing yourself, you can make changes in the mind, the personality and in your human nature. You can change any habit or personality trait, regardless of how embedded it is, through discipline. In fact, great resistance offers even greater potential for true and lasting change. Keep up daily practices, come what may, and Awareness will be integrated into the very matrix of your life.

The goal is not perfecting the yogic practices. They are simply a *sadhana*, a toolbox, a means to the goal, which is awareness. When the practices are no longer an exertion and have become a way of life, you will have established "a new" way of living. You will see in every moment where you are present an opportunity to make spiritual progress. You will begin a life that lives to grow and perfect itself, and all of your day-to-day experiences will become a field for your perfection. Your life will become your Yoga and you will realize that "action with awareness" was not only the vehicle of your transformation, it is your destination.

For information on Babaji's Kriya Yoga please contact:

Babaji's Kriya Yoga and Publications, Inc.
196 Mountain Road • P.O. Box 90
Eastman, Quebec • Canada J0E 1P0
Tel: +1(888) 252-9642 • +1(450) 297-0258 • Fax: +1(450) 297-3957
www.babajiskriyayoga.net • info@babajiskriyayoga.net

ABOUT THE AUTHORS

Durga Jan Ahlund has been practicing and studying Yoga since 1967, and teaching Yoga regularly, since 1990. She teaches Hatha Yoga, Kundalini Yoga, Kriya Yoga and also practices as a Yoga therapist. She created a two year self-study course on Yoga and Meditation and wrote, acted and produced the video, "Kriya Hatha Yoga: Self-realization through Action with Awareness." She has written a book on Kriya Yoga, "Insight Along the Path," with Marshall Govindan. She developed and has been teaching since 1998, a 200-hour Hatha Yoga Teacher Training Course (Yoga Alliance certified) at the Kriya Yoga Ashram in Quebec, and in India, Brazil and Europe. She has been involved in the editing of many Yoga books for Kriya Yoga Order of Acharyas and Kriya Yoga Publications. She was inducted into the teaching Order of Acharyas of Babaji's Kriya Yoga in Bangalore, India in January 2003 and gives Initiations into Babaji's Kriya Yoga in Canada and the U.S.A. She is married to Marshall Govindan Satchidananda and has two grown sons. She can be reached at: durga@babajiskriyayoga.net

Marshall Govindan Satchidananda has practiced Babaji's Kriya Yoga intensively since 1969. He studied and practiced Kriya Yoga in India for five years with Yogi S.A.A. Ramaiah, assisting him in the establishment of 23 yoga centers around the world during an 18 year period as a dedicated. During this period he practiced Kriya Yoga for eight hours per day on average, and as a result attained Self-realization.

While in India he studied the Tamil language and the works of the Tamil Yoga Siddhas. In 1980 he assisted in the collection and publication of the complete writings of Siddhar Boganathar in Tamil. In 1988 he was asked by Babaji Nagaraj, the founder of Kriya Yoga to begin teaching. In 1991, he wrote the best selling book, "Babaji and the 18 Siddha Kriya Yoga Tradition", now published in 11 languages. In 1992 he founded Babaji's Kriya Yoga Ashram on a beautiful 80 acre mountain top site in St. Etienne de Bolton, Quebec. He offers classes, seminars and retreats there year round. In 1993, he edited and published the first international English translation of "Tirumandiram: a Classic of Yoga and Tantra."

In 1995 he retired from a 25 year career as an economist and later a systems auditor to devote himself full time to teaching and publishing in the field of Yoga. Since 1992, he has travelled extensively throughout the world guiding about many Kriya Yoga study groups in over 20 countries, ashrams in Canada and Bangalore, India, and a lay order of teachers of Kriya Yoga: Babaji's Kriya Yoga Order of Acharyas, a non-profit educational charity, incorporated in the USA, Canada and India. Since 1989 he has personally initiated over 7,500 persons in Babaji's Kriya Yoga in a series of intensive sessions and retreats.

From 2000 to 2001, he completed the writing of, and publication of "Kriya Yoga Sutras of Patanjali and the Siddhas," in several European languages. Since 2000, he has co-sponsored with Dr. Georg Feuerstein, Ph.D., a team of scholars in a large scale research project engaged in the preservation, transcription, translation and publication of the whole of the literature related to the Yoga of the 18 Siddhas.

The Grace of Babaji's Kriya Yoga

A Course of Lessons

An Invitation from Babaji's Kriya Yoga and Publications, Inc.

Two years of Self- Exploration & Discovery

"To hope for a change in human life without a change in human nature is an irrational & un-spiritual proposition; it is to ask for something unnatural & unreal, an impossible miracle." Sri Aurobindo

In our pursuit of our Divine Self we must seek for change in our human nature. But rather than trying to change our nature, we more often merely attempt to reconcile our habits of desire, aversion and fear. So dark elements along with light con-tinue to seek manifestation and arise in the context of our life.

The Grace Course provokes us to delve into our desires, aversions and fears in order to reveal to us our truth and falseness.

As ingrained habits and instincts are probed, weaknesses will be amplified. This process is personal and profound and real work.

Have You Sincerely and Genuinely Considered:

☐ How far can discipline and personal effort get you?
☐ What is Grace and is it absolutely necessary for Self-Knowledge?
☐ Is your Ego really so bad?
☐ Must I love everyone, or just do my duty?
☐ How can I keep love from diminishing into attachment or dissolving into anger or indifference?
☐ Why is life so full of desire, aversion and fear?
☐ Is there ever a need for fear?
☐ How can I learn to use my willpower effectively to overcome my resistances?
☐ Is there a Higher Will for my life, and if so, how can I learn to connect with it?
☐ Is what you can "see," even in meditation, ever the true Self?

The entire course consists of 24 monthly lessons. Each lesson is about 15 pages. You may subscribe one year at a time: $108 per year

To subscribe to this course, contact us at: **Babaji's Kriya Yoga Publications**

196 Mountain Road　PO Box 90　Eastman　QC　J0E 1P0　Canada
www.babajiskriyayoga.net

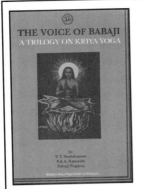

THE VOICE OF BABAJI
A TRILOGY ON KRIYA YOGA

Sri V.T. Neelakantan recorded verbatim a series of talks given by Satguru Kriya Babaji in 1953. These are a fountain of delight and inspiration, illuminating the Kriya Yoga path towards God realization, unity in diversity and universal love. They also reveal the magnetic personality of Babaji and how he supports us all, with much humour and wisdom. 216 pages, 4 maps, Includes the fascinating accounts of the meetings with Babaji in Madras and in the Himalayas by authors V.T. Neelakantan and Yogi S.A.A. Ramaiah. Out of print for nearly 50 years, they are profound and important statements from one of the world's greatest living spiritual masters. 8 pages in color. 534 pages. ISBN 978-1-895383-23-2. Canada: CAD$41.19, USA: US$33.00, Asia & Europe: US$58.50

Prices include shipping charges

THE WISDOM OF JESUS AND THE YOGA SIDDHA

by Marshall Govindan

Who was Jesus? One of the most influential human beings of all times? The founder of Christianity? A messiah or savior sent by God to redeem humanity of its sins? What were His teachings? Is our knowledge of Jesus limited to what is recorded in the Bible? What has modern historical research to say about what Jesus did and taught? "What were the original teachings of Jesus, before the Christian religion became organized?" 224 pages, soft cover 6" x 9". ISBN 978-1-895383-43-0. Canada: CAD$22.93, USA: US$20.45, Asia & Europe: US$31.40

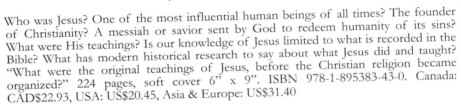

BABAJI and the 18 Siddha Kriya Yoga Tradition
8th Edition

by M. Govindan

A rare account of Babaji, the Himalayan master who developed Kriya Yoga, the Siddhas, his source of inspiration and the principles of Kriya Yoga. Guidelines for its practice. 216 pages, 4 maps, 33 color photos, 100 bibliographic references and glossary. Soft cover 6" x 9".
ISBN 978-1-895383-00-3. Canada: CAD$25.81, USA: US$21.45, Asia & Europe: US$32.40

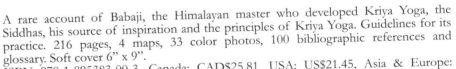

KRIYA YOGA: INSIGHTS ALONG THE PATH

by M. Govindan and Jan Ahlund

My wife, Jan "Durga" Ahlund and I have recognized for many years the need for a book that would explain to both those interested in learning Kriya Yoga and those already embarked on its path, why they should practice it, what are the difficulties, and how to overcome them. We believe that this book will help prepare everyone for the challenges and opportunities that Kriya Yoga provides.
ISBN 978-1-895383-49-2. Canada: CAD$19.78, USA: US$18.50, Asia & Europe: US$29.45

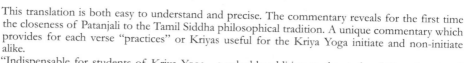
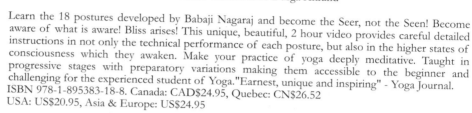